LET TECHNOLOGY DO THE WORK

A Step By Step Guide to Automating Reports

Eva Madison

Let Technology Do the Work
www.lettechnologydothework.com
Copyright © 2017-2018 Eva Madison

First Paperback Edition printed 2017

ISBN: 978-1-77277-156-5

Limits of Liability and Disclaimer of Warranty
The author and publisher shall not be liable for your misuse of the enclosed material. This book is strictly for informational and educational purposes only.

Warning – Disclaimer
The purpose of this book is to educate and entertain. The author and/or publisher do not guarantee that anyone following these techniques, suggestions, tips, ideas, or strategies will become successful. The author and/or publisher shall have neither liability nor responsibility to anyone with respect to any loss or damage caused, or alleged to be caused, directly or indirectly by the information contained in this book.

The author is not affiliated with Microsoft in any way. Microsoft, Excel, Visual Basic, Access, SharePoint and Windows are registered trademarks of Microsoft Corporation in the U.S. and other countries. Other brand names and product names mentioned in this book are trademarks of service marks of their respective companies.

Medical Disclaimer
The medical or health information in this book is provided as an information resource only, and is not to be used or relied on for any diagnostic or treatment purposes. This information is not intended to be patient education, does not create any patient-physician relationship, and should not be used as a substitute for professional diagnosis and treatment.

Publisher
10-10-10 Publishing
Markham, ON Canada
Printed in Canada and the United States of America

Table of Contents

Acknowledgements

I am extremely fortunate to have the support and guidance of many amazing people. I would like to express my sincere gratitude to:

Benn Konsynski for your valuable guidance, insight and continuous support.

Jon Congdon for encouraging me to write this book.

Mike Aysan for always being available to provide guidance.

Joy Marshall for all of your advice and friendship throughout the years.

My husband, Todd Madison, for always supporting me and helping me when I need it the most.

My mom, Mary Dimitrov, for being a wonderful, supportive, loving mom.

My brother, Adam Dimitrov, for always encouraging me and leading by example.

Testimonials

Eva's background in audit and financial reporting is ideal for providing reporting solutions. In this book she brings a unique perspective to a common problem that plagues financial leadership. She has the ability to take complex problems and provide easy, sustainable solutions that have an immediate impact on the informational value of an organization's financial reporting.

Kerry Buchan

Eva introduced me to her streamlined system a year ago. I saw an immediate improvement in my daily organization and ability to leave work at the office since everything was captured. One year later, my overall efficiency has increased 100%. I now have more work life balance and have been able to take on stretch goals at work. Eva's tools are amazing!

Beth Massengill

Foreword

I am pleased to introduce you to Eva Madison, author of the book *Let Technology Do the Work*. Eva has provided you with an easy-to-follow, step-by-step guide to automating reports in order to save time and money in your business. You will also learn different techniques that you can use to automate your home life as well.

Eva's experience and passion are clearly visible in this book. She takes a normally intimidating and complex issue that is present in your company, and provides a solution that is easy for you to understand and apply. Not only will Eva teach you her strategies for automating your business, but she will also walk you through how to quantify the benefits of these techniques, so that you can put a number on just how much time and money you will save!

Let Technology Do the Work reaches past automating reports in order to help you to become more effective, both at work and at home! It is sure to become a must read, as the importance of managing data and data quality continues to rise in your business.

Read *Let Technology Do the Work* today and discover how to automate your work to save valuable time and money!

Raymond Aaron
New York Times Bestselling Author

1
LET'S CHANGE OUR FOCUS

ROUTINE VS. STRATEGIC TASKS

When routine tasks take up the majority of the day, it's difficult to focus on the strategic tasks that have a greater impact on our lives. Routine tasks are tasks that you perform often but don't personally add a lot of value to by doing them. For example, running a report and waiting 4 hours for it to download, combining data when a system could combine it for you, running back and forth to the dry cleaner or grocery store, etc. In contrast, strategic tasks are tasks that can greatly impact our lives like writing books, going back to school, or researching how to solve complex problems at work. These are tasks that you personally add a lot of value to, are the only person who can do them, and/or that you really enjoy doing. The goal of this book is to help you reduce the amount of time spent on routine tasks in order to preserve the energy and clarity you need to work on strategic tasks.

Ideally, you'll begin to shift from the current state to the optimal state. You'll always do routine tasks, but the goal is to minimize the time you spend doing them.

Current State

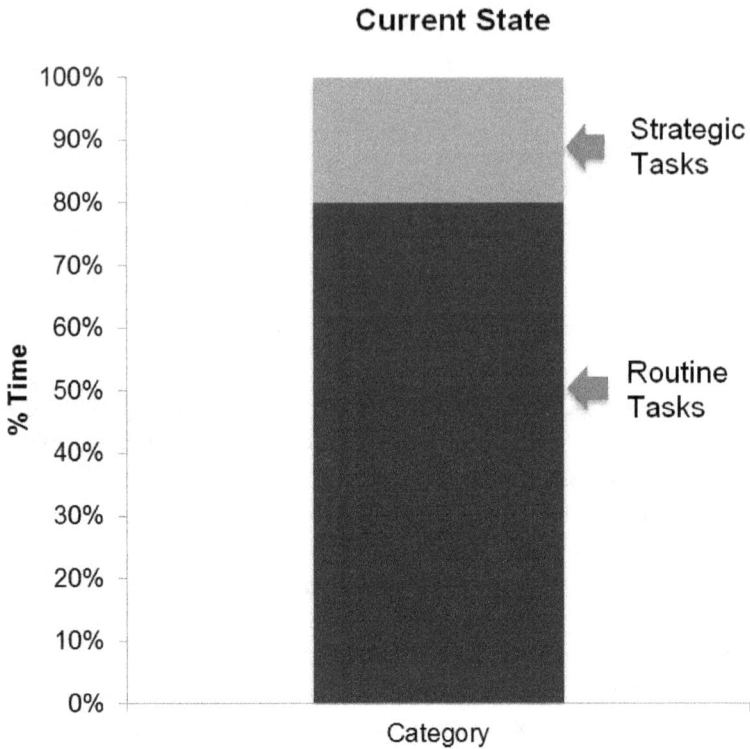

Current State
Characteristics: 80% Routine, 20% Strategic

- Feeling like you are forgetting to do something
- Stressing about tomorrow
- Feeling unprepared/not having time to prepare
- Feeling like there are not enough hours in the day
- Feeling defeated
- Analysis paralysis
- Not calm
- Exhausted

Optimal State

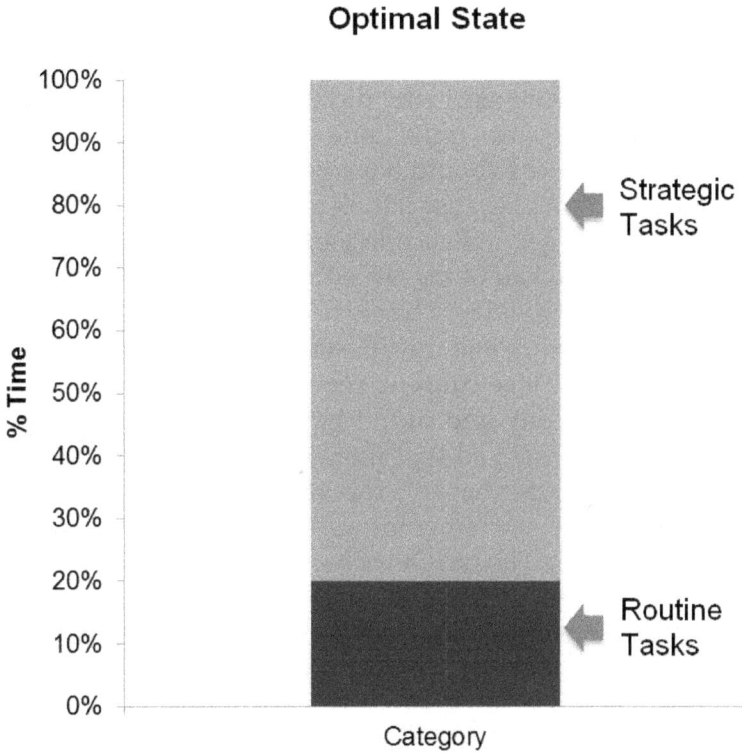

Optimal State
Characteristics: 80% Strategic, 20% Routine

- Feeling calm
- Feeling in control
- Knowing that everything is taken care of
- Carefree
- Successful in meetings
- Healthy
- Energetic
- Helpful

WHY I BEGAN TO SHIFT TO THE OPTIMAL STAGE

For several months, every time I submitted a report at work, someone would always ask "why did this increase" or "are you sure these numbers are right" and I would suddenly feel overwhelmed. I knew I should have been able to answer these questions but couldn't because it took me so long to compile this report that I didn't get a chance to look at the variances. I also hoped that I followed all of the steps to combine the data so the report was correct. One day, I wrote down all of my tasks that I was performing at work and the time that it took me to complete them. I found that I was running reports and combining data the majority of the day and didn't have any time left over to analyze the data. I realized that this had to change so I began figuring out how to automate the reports and saw a benefit right away! Soon, people started coming to me asking me how to automate their work. The next few chapters are filled with ideas for reducing the time it takes to run reports while increasing consistency and accuracy. First, let's walk through some real life examples where automating reports can help.

THE BENEFITS

EXAMPLE 1: AUTOMATING THE REPORT

One day, I was on the phone talking to a co-worker who mentioned that he had to come in at 5am every Wednesday to start running reports for a 9am meeting. I asked him to walk me through what he does on these mornings. It turned out that he ran several reports that took hours to download, and he had to wait for one report to finish before he could start the next report. Then he emailed these large reports to everyone right before the 9am meeting and always had issues with people receiving the reports because they were too large. He had been doing this for years.

After walking through a few alternatives, we talked to a colleague in our IT department and asked them to schedule the reports to automatically run after midnight and to deliver them to the SharePoint site so the reports didn't fill everyone's email. This took us about two hours to solve and now he no longer comes in at 5am to run reports! *Time savings: 4 hours per week and not having to come in at 5am*

EXAMPLE 2: COMBINING METRICS

I inherited a package of metrics that took about a week to run and I was always having a really hard time meeting the deadline. Since this was a weekly report, this became the only file that I could work on. It was a critical management tool so I was doing everything possible to meet the deadline. The data for this file was coming from multiple sources: several reports, emails from different departments, keying data in to an Excel file, etc. Most of the data in the supporting documents rolled up to one scorecard but, because the data in the supporting documents was inconsistent, I had to roll the scorecard up manually. The time frames of the reports didn't match so the report was not very accurate. After the process was automated, I reduced the time from 1 week to 4 hours! *Time savings: 36 hours per week and I could work on other projects.*

Reports: Combined using Access
- Accessed a read only table that housed operational metrics
- Created an import method for the data that couldn't be accessed through a table
- Created a hierarchy table
- Created reference tables for all sources and mapped them to the hierarchy
- Created an output table in order to move data to the Excel file

Department Scorecards
- Changed the process so files were uploaded to a central location (not through email)
- Worked with each person and mapped the data on each report so I could roll the data up easily

Excel
- Created tabs for all inputs (output from Access, department scorecards, etc.)
- Mapped all tabs to the scorecard

Chapters two through five will walk you through how to perform these steps.

EXAMPLE 3: ACCURACY OF DATA

I was working with a new team and one of the team members mentioned that he was going to work on his vacation because he had to manually move data from one system to another. He said that he does this every Tuesday night and Wednesday morning. I asked him to walk me through his process in detail while I documented the steps in a process map (see Chapter 2, Visualize the Process and Quantify Savings). He downloaded data from an expense system into Excel and then uploaded it into a billing system. If he received an error message when he uploaded the file, then he would manually change the data in the Excel file and try to upload it again. After looking into the changes that he was making, I realized that he was changing client codes, which could result in expenses being billed to the wrong clients.

I needed to fix this quickly, so I built a file in Access that took the data from the expense system, checked for inconsistent data, and displayed error tables when the data didn't match. This gave me the information that I needed to follow up with the project managers. If the entry was correct, I created a unique identifier and then ran output tables to import into the billing system. I no longer received errors when I uploaded the data and the data was accurate. I then changed the billing system so it could receive the right layer of data from the expense system, which permanently solved the problem. *Time savings: 7 hours per week.*

SHIFT THE EFFORT

The effort shouldn't be in creating the report; it should be on analyzing the data. The accuracy and consistency of reports that are not automated at the source are dependent on the person, or people, that are running them. The best-case scenario is to work with IT to automate the reports and have them delivered to your inbox without any manual manipulation.

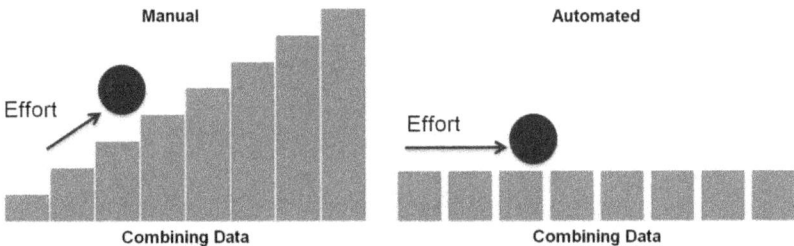

But what do you do if data is housed in multiple systems or if IT is unable to allocate resources to automate it for you? Or if you are not sure about what you need and need time to develop a solution? That is what we will cover in the next few chapters!

There are several programs that IT has access to, such as SQL Server, that would be amazing for us to work with. Unfortunately, these systems are expensive and carry some risk as users can create their own island of data that is not supported by IT. One suite of programs that is pretty standard on our work issued computers is the Microsoft package, which contains Excel and Access. These programs are powerful and go a long way to automate and streamline reports and tasks. Handing files off to other people to run, or helping people automate their files is easier in Excel and Access since most people have some level of familiarity with these programs.

So, let's learn how to automate. Chapters two through five will walk you through how to automate reports in order to reduce the amount of time spent on routine tasks. I'll discuss how to visualize the process, adjust the current reports to meet your needs, automate using Excel and Access, as well as how to continuously improve your system. Please keep in mind that this book teaches you how to combine data and reports and is not intended to be a tutorial for Excel or Access.

In chapters six and seven I'll provide tips that have helped me manage my time better at work and home. Visit my website at www.lettechnologydothework.com for detailed files and updated tips.

NOTES

_____

_____

_____

_____

_____

_____

_____

_____

_____

_____

_____

_____

_____

_____

_____

_____

_____

_____

2
VISUALIZE THE PROCESS AND QUANTIFY SAVINGS

Drawing the process helps me to visualize the entire process and easily identify waste or unnecessary steps. This normally includes downloading a report out of a system, any data manipulation, the people involved in developing the report, and who receives the final product. Once I am finished drawing the process, I can usually remove several steps *BEFORE* automating the report by reassigning tasks to different employees. Then I calculate the time spent at each step before and after automation in order to quantify the savings of changing the process.

There are 6 steps in visualizing the process and quantifying savings:

1. Walk through the process
2. Draw the process by task or person
3. Add details
4. Add time and cost
5. Analyze
6. Calculate Savings

STEP 1: WALK THROUGH THE PROCESS

In order to walk through the process, find the person that starts the process and interview them. Document the source and purpose of the request, the frequency, the steps that they take to perform their part, how long each task takes them, and what they do with the file or report. Ask them to log in and perform every step while you are interviewing them because people accidently leave steps out when they just describe the process from memory. Remember to ask for screen prints and files so you can refer to them when you are completing your documentation. This can also become a training tool for the person who may end up taking on a different part of the process.

STEP 2: DRAW THE PROCESS BY TASK OR PERSON

There are two ways that I like to draw the process.

1. Separate major tasks: process includes 1 or 2 people.
2. Separate tasks by person: process includes more than 2 people.

Separating the process by major tasks allows you to see if you can automate and remove steps for the person running the process. For example, if one person downloads a report, adds formulas to it in Excel and emails it to another person, the process would look like this:

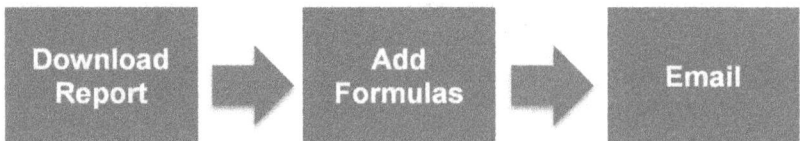

Separating the tasks by person will enable you to not only remove steps but to also remove people from the process. It is also beneficial because it shows exactly what each person is responsible for. In theory, the fewer people that touch the report and the more you can automate, the quicker the process will be.

Every manual manipulation leaves room for errors and inconsistencies. At the end of the day, we are looking to be more efficient and accurate. For example, Person 1 runs a report and sends it to Person 2, Person 2 adds year to date data and sends it to Person 3, Person 3 adds a reporting structure and sends it to Person 4, Person 4 adds waterfalls and comments and sends it to Person 5, and Person 5 populates the scorecard and sends it to Person 6. This process would look like this:

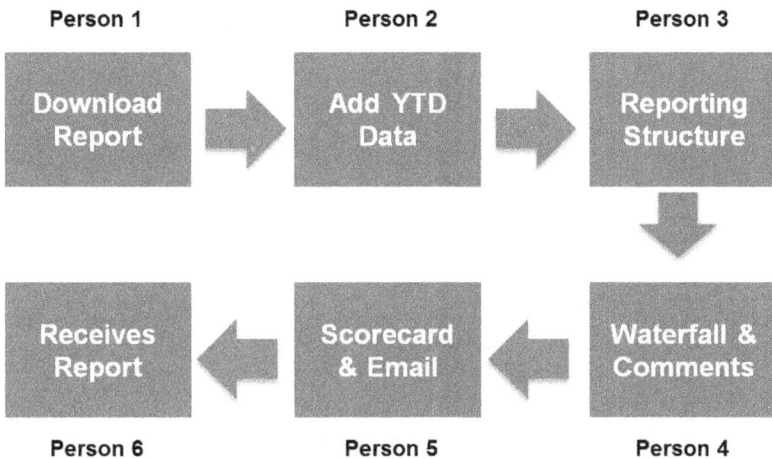

Person 1		Person 2		Person 3
Download Report	→	**Add YTD Data**	→	**Reporting Structure**

Person 6		Person 5		Person 4
Receives Report	←	**Scorecard & Email**	←	**Waterfall & Comments**

STEP 3: ADD DETAILS

Document the steps that are performed in as much detail as possible in order to be able to duplicate them. This will also help you when you try to automate reports with IT as you will be able to show them exactly what you are looking for. For example, if the report is run from System X, the details will include the following information: Login to System X > click on the reporting tab > accounting and finance folder > report name: Sales by Region Report > change filter to current month and year > select export to Excel > Save in Finance Drive/Sales by Region folder.

STEP 4: ADD TIME AND COST

When I am walking through the process, I always document the time that it takes to perform the task. Then, I estimate the rate per hour to determine the cost of performing that step.

STEP 5: ANALYZE

The goal is to reduce the number of times that the process changes hands and to identify key points within the process. Parts in the process that normally cannot be automated represent key points. For example, on the previous page, the key point is the Waterfall and Comments node (Person 4) as this information usually resides with a person and, most of the time, cannot be automated. When evaluating a process, consider the following:

1. What is the end product? Does the end product need to be revisited?
2. Where are the key points in the process?
3. Can you combine steps?
4. Where are the manual steps? Can you automate them?
5. Will combining any steps cause a segregation of duties issue (internal control issue)?

STEP 6: CALCULATE SAVINGS

This step is similar to Step 4. Step 4 is calculated before the process has been changed and this step is calculated after the process has been changed. This will represent your cost savings.

Let's walk through two examples. Example 1 will be separated by major task and Example 2 will separate tasks by person. Let's start with the first example.

TYPE 1: SEPARATE BY MAJOR TASK
Example 1: Sales And Credits By Location

STEP 1: WALK THROUGH THE PROCESS

One person combines data from two reports, each from a different system, and creates a scorecard. The scorecard shows sales and credits by location.

- Run Report 1, Total Sales, and download it to Excel. Approximately 1 hour for it to download. *Time 1 hour 10 minutes.*

- Report 1. Sort and remove all rows where the total is equal to $0. *Time 10 minutes.*

- Report 1. Summarize by location. *Time 10 minutes.*

- Run Report 2, Total Credits, and download it to Excel. Approximately 30 minutes for it to download. *Time 40 minutes.*

- Report 2. Sort and add a year to date calculation. *Time 10 minutes.*

- Report 2. Summarize by location. *Time 10 minutes.*

- Create a scorecard showing results from Report 1 and Report 2. *Time 30 minutes.*

- Email to department because the group has not been created in the email system. *Time 10 minutes.*

STEP 2: DRAW THE PROCESS BY TASK

The process would look like this:

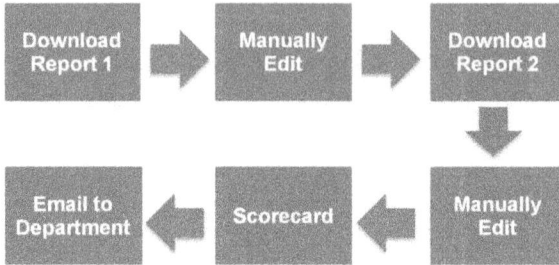

Download Report 1	→	Manually Edit	→	Download Report 2

Email to Department	←	Scorecard	←	Manually Edit

STEP 3: ADD DETAILS

Now, let's add the details.

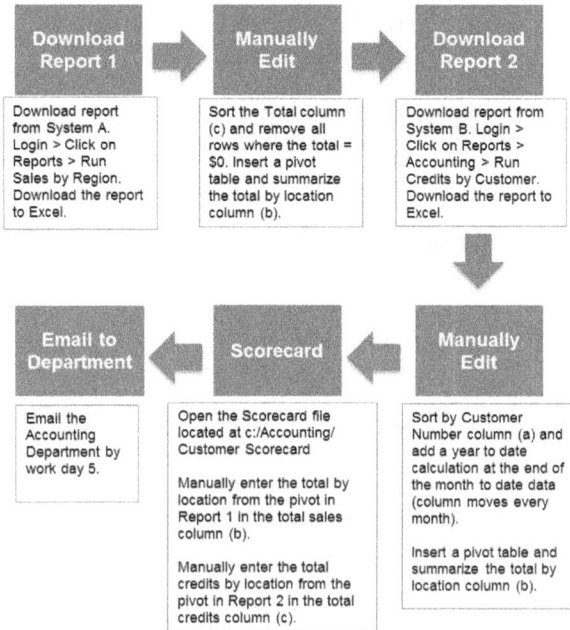

Download Report 1	→	Manually Edit	→	Download Report 2
Download report from System A. Login > Click on Reports > Run Sales by Region. Download the report to Excel.		Sort the Total column (c) and remove all rows where the total = $0. Insert a pivot table and summarize the total by location column (b).		Download report from System B. Login > Click on Reports > Accounting > Run Credits by Customer. Download the report to Excel.

Email to Department	←	Scorecard	←	Manually Edit
Email the Accounting Department by work day 5.		Open the Scorecard file located at c:/Accounting/ Customer Scorecard. Manually enter the total by location from the pivot in Report 1 in the total sales column (b). Manually enter the total credits by location from the pivot in Report 2 in the total credits column (c).		Sort by Customer Number column (a) and add a year to date calculation at the end of the month to date data (column moves every month). Insert a pivot table and summarize the total by location column (b).

Please visit www.LetTechnologyDoTheWork.com for full image.

STEP 4: ADD TIME AND COST

Calculate the cost of each task.

#	Task	Time (Minutes)	Time (Hours)	Rate/ Hour	Cost
1	Download Report 1 and save in Excel	70	1.2	70	$ 82
2	Report 1: Sort and Remove Rows	10	0.2	70	$ 12
3	Report 1: Summarize by Location	10	0.2	70	$ 12
4	Download Report 2 and save in Excel	40	0.7	70	$ 47
5	Report 2: Sort and add Year to Date Calc	10	0.2	70	$ 12
6	Report 2: Summarize by Location	10	0.2	70	$ 12
7	Populate Scorecard	30	0.5	70	$ 35
8	Email to department	10	0.2	70	$ 12
		190	3.4		$ 224

STEP 5: ANALYZE

This is the fun part! Let's see what changes we can make to reduce the amount of time that it takes to complete the process.

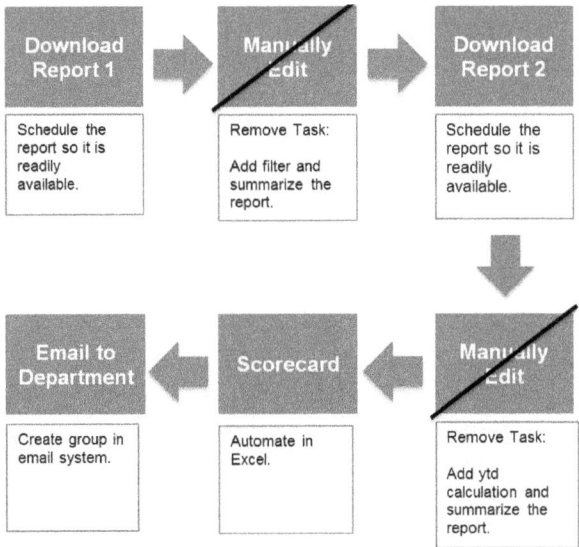

STEP 6: CALCULATE SAVINGS

Calculate the savings based on the changes made in Step 5.

#	Task	Time (Minutes)	Time (Hours)	Rate/ Hour	Cost
1	Download Report 1 and save in Excel	5	0.1	70	$ 6
2	Report 1: Sort and Remove Rows	0	-	70	$ -
3	Report 1: Summarize by Location	0	-	70	$ -
4	Download Report 2 and save in Excel	5	0.1	70	$ 6
5	Report 2: Sort and add Year to Date Calc	0	-	70	$ -
6	Report 2: Summarize by Location	0	-	70	$ -
7	Populate Scorecard	10	0.2	70	$ 12
8	Email to department	2	0.0	70	$ 2
		22	0.4		$ 26

We were able to reduce the amount of time from 3.4 hours to 22 minutes and saved $198 every month by just making a few minor changes to the process (88% time savings).

Savings	Before	After	Savings
Time (minutes)	190	22	168
Cost Savings	$ 224	$ 26	$ 198

This is just a simple example, but I have automated reports that have saved over 120 hours a month, so the savings can be significant. Also, the opportunity for human errors is dramatically reduced.

Now, let's walk through the second type and separate tasks by person.

TYPE 2 – SEPARATE TASKS BY PERSON
Example 2: Sales By Region

STEP 1: WALK THROUGH THE PROCESS

The following process represents a simplified reporting request. Let's say that a sales manager requests a report that describes the year over year changes by region. Sales by region is maintained in System A by month. The year to date information is available; however, the report that is being used to combine this data is a month to date report. Even though the company reassigned regions late last year, the systems have not been updated; however, the sales manager would like the updates reflected in the report. The information also needs to be added to the scorecard and all changes greater than 5% need to be highlighted. Since this report includes multiple people, let's separate the tasks by person.

- Person 1: Downloads the Sales by Region Report from System A for the month of October. *Time 20 minutes.*

- Person 2: Adds the data from January – September and a calculation that sums the year to date data in Excel. *Time 50 minutes.*

- Person 3: Adds a tab in Excel that maps the regions differently because the regions that are included in the system are outdated. All of the reference formulas need to be adjusted in the file. *Time 60 minutes.*

- Person 4: Adds a waterfall chart and comments on the year to date changes. *Time 120 minutes.*

- Person 5: Adds the amount from October to the scorecard. All reference formulas need to be added again because all of the calculations were removed from last month's scorecard so the manager didn't change them by accident and distort the report. *Time 40 minutes.*

- Person 6: Is really only interested in the year to date changes, but reviews all of the information because it has been provided. *Time 90 minutes.*

STEP 2: DRAW THE PROCESS BY PERSON

The process would look like this:

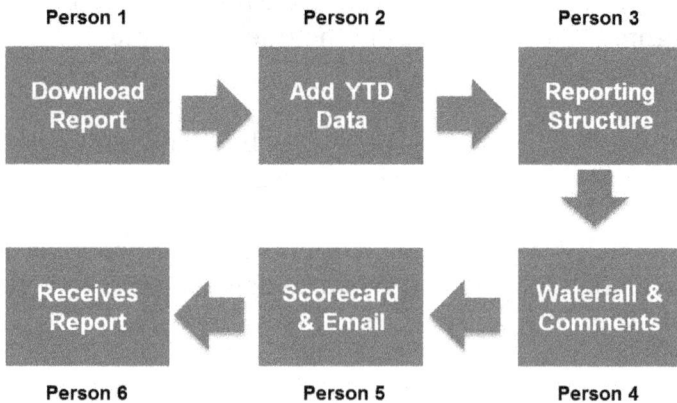

Person 1	Person 2	Person 3
Download Report	Add YTD Data	Reporting Structure

Receives Report	Scorecard & Email	Waterfall & Comments
Person 6	Person 5	Person 4

STEP 3: ADD DETAILS

Now, let's add the details

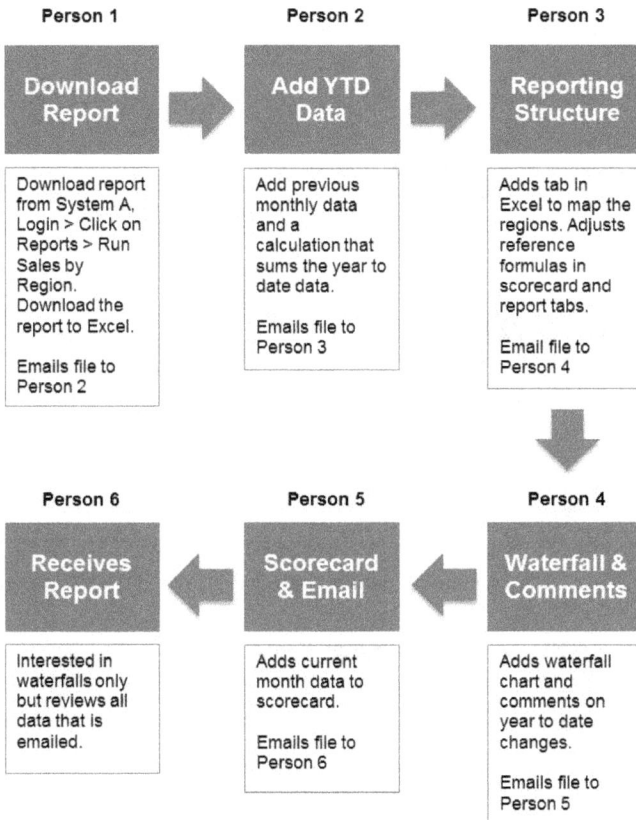

Person 1	Person 2	Person 3
Download Report	**Add YTD Data**	**Reporting Structure**
Download report from System A. Login > Click on Reports > Run Sales by Region. Download the report to Excel. Emails file to Person 2	Add previous monthly data and a calculation that sums the year to date data. Emails file to Person 3	Adds tab in Excel to map the regions. Adjusts reference formulas in scorecard and report tabs. Email file to Person 4

Person 6	Person 5	Person 4
Receives Report	**Scorecard & Email**	**Waterfall & Comments**
Interested in waterfalls only but reviews all data that is emailed.	Adds current month data to scorecard. Emails file to Person 6	Adds waterfall chart and comments on year to date changes. Emails file to Person 5

STEP 4: ADD TIME AND COST

Calculate the cost of each person that is working on the report.

Person	Action	Time (Minutes)	Time (Hours)	Rate/ Hour	Cost
1	Downloads a report from System A	20	0.3	45	$ 15
2	Adds year to date data	50	0.8	65	$ 54
3	Adds the reporting structure	60	1.0	65	$ 65
4	Adds waterfall graphs & comments	120	2.0	80	$ 160
5	Adds the data to a scorecard	40	0.7	80	$ 53
6	Person 6 reviews the data	90	1.5	200	$ 300
		380	6.3		$ 647

STEP 5: ANALYZE

Let's consider the following changes:

• Update the reporting structure in System A.

• Add the reporting structure and year to date data to the report and schedule it to run and deliver automatically.

• Remove the scorecard because no one is using it.

These steps remove 4 people from the process! Going forward, the report will be delivered to Person 4 who will add the waterfall and comments. The waterfall charts can be automated (we'll discuss automating graphs in Chapter 4, Automate in Excel) but researching variances and adding comments normally cannot, which is what makes this a key point.

Now, let's look at our savings.

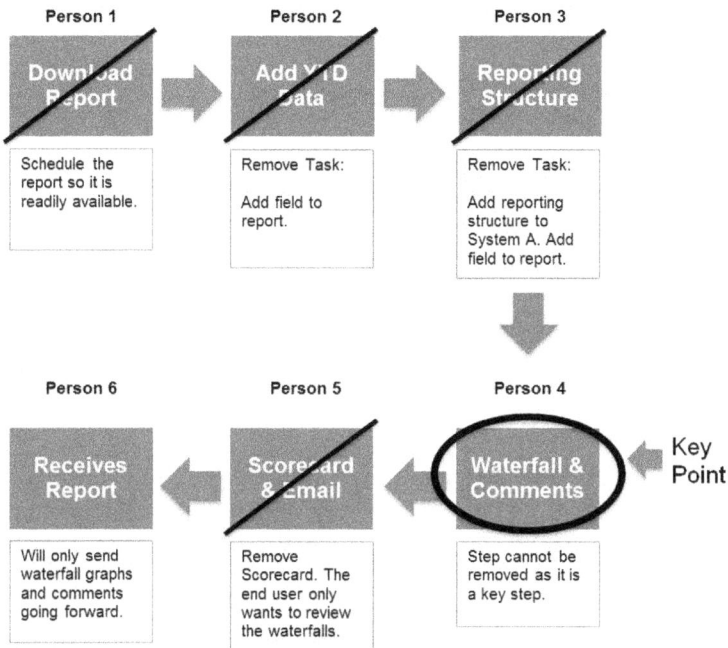

STEP 6: CALCULATE SAVINGS

Calculate the savings based on changes made in Step 5.

Person	Action	Time (Minutes)	Time (Hours)	Rate/ Hour		Cost
1	Downloads a report from System A	0	-	45	$	-
2	Adds year to date data	0	-	65	$	-
3	Adds the reporting structure	0	-	65	$	-
4	Adds waterfall graphs & comments	120	2.0	80	$	160
5	Adds the data to a scorecard	0	-	80	$	-
6	Person 6 reviews the data	20	0.3	200	$	67
		140	2.3		$	227

We were able to reduce the amount of time by 4 hours and saved $420 every month by making a few minor changes to the process (63% time savings).

Savings	Before	After	Savings
Time (minutes)	380	140	240
Cost Savings	$ 647	$ 227	$ 420

The time is reduced significantly because fewer people are involved, all of the data is readily available and the process is continuous (not picked and put back down by multiple people).

Now that we've discussed visualizing the process and calculating savings in detail, let's move on to automating reports in Chapter 3, Adjust the Reports First!

NOTES

3
ADJUST THE REPORTS FIRST

The first thing to consider when you are automating a process that includes reports is how you can adjust the reports so they come directly out of the system without further manual manipulation. It is better to let the system do the work for you than it is to automate the manual steps. Automating the report will allow you to eliminate steps and reduce costs, which was the goal of Chapter 2, Visualize the Process and Quantify Savings.

The benefits of adjusting the reports include less time to process and better accuracy of data. Adjusting the reports also give users visibility into the data and helps to reduce scatter, meaning the data in all of the reports that everybody pulls is the same. It is very frustrating to receive multiple reports that should contain the same data and the totals are different. A lot of time is spent trying to figure out why these totals are different. If the data is updated properly in the system, then the likelihood that the data will match significantly increases. Being able to reach end users is important because it allows them to run the reports when needed instead of waiting on someone else to produce the report.

Usually, in systems, there are two ways to save reports. The first way is to save it to your personal folder where only you can see and run the reports. This option is a great option if you have sensitive data, you are the only person producing a report with the data, or the report is in draft form. The second way to save a report is to make the report public so everyone is running the same report. This option is used for reports that are run by multiple people and is very helpful in containing the scatter as everyone is running the report with the same filters and information. It also allows users to run the report on demand.

Two potential downfalls to watch out for when sharing reports:

1. Access rights can change the data that is displayed.
2. People can download the report and manipulate it so the numbers change.

Access rights issues are usually pretty easy to identify but you can't control if someone else manipulates the report after they run it. When I find scatter, I find it beneficial to sit with the user to understand why the data is being manipulated and see if we can incorporate the changes into the report. Often, you can add an extra column with a different calculation and then the report meets everyone's needs.

Creating or adjusting reports in some systems can be intuitive. In these systems, ask for reporting access so you can edit the report, save it to your personal folder and then add the fields. Perform checks against batch totals in the system or other reports to ensure the data is accurate. Remember to consider who else is using the report before overwriting it because you can affect their downstream process. For the systems that are not intuitive, it's better to get IT involved. Following are some tips for working with IT or for creating reports on your own:

1. Explain the end product; IT may have better ways of getting there or know what data is not accurate in the system.

2. Using the process details from Chapter 2, Visualize the Process and Quantify Savings, explain the data that needs to be added to the current reports (user requirements).

3. If you want to add a field that you see on the screen, provide a screen shot of the field. Nearly every field that you see on a screen is saved in a table making it accessible by the report writing feature. Some field names are not intuitive, which causes issues when you are trying to find them in the report writer. For instance, a customer name field may be called LFKO in the reporting suite. As a user, unless you know the system, this would take a long time to figure out. IT is able to access the configuration area and quickly figure out what each field is called.

4. If you find yourself downloading a report and adding calculations to it, add the calculations directly to the report. There are two ways to do this:

    a) Most reporting suites have a calculation field where you can calculate items that are already displayed on the report. This is the most common option.

    b) Add the calculation to the database so it can be accessed on any report.

5. If I need to manipulate a report, I usually download it as .csv instead of .xlsx. When you download a report in Excel (.xlsx), it usually includes headers and will sometimes include page breaks (a blank row between data). When you download a report as a .csv, the page breaks disappear, making it easier to manipulate the data.

6. Ask IT if they can schedule a report. I have found a few ways to deliver reports that are very helpful: email, folders within

the system, or an intranet site. For example, the same report that you run and wait for an hour to download from the system can be scheduled to run and be delivered automatically. This can save you hours of processing time!

7. There are usually two layers of data (sometimes more) that you need to consider when creating a report. These layers are called different names in different systems, but I will refer to them as a summary layer and a detail layer. The summary layer normally includes high level information, like customer totals, reports totals, etc. The detailed layer includes totals by each detailed line item.

Expense Report

Report ID	145000
Date	1/10/2018
Total of Report	$ 1,500

Line item ID	Date	Type	Amount
1a	1/5/2018	Meal	$ 50
1b	1/10/2018	Hotel	$ 450
1c	1/7/2018	Training	$ 1,000
			$ 1,500

Combing data from different layers will sometimes result in duplicate data. If you find that adding a field to a report makes the report inaccurate, then create two reports, add the same field to each report, summarize them, and combine them using Excel (See Chapter 4, Automate in Excel for details). If you create two reports, ensure that the periods match so you don't combine data from different periods.

For example, let's say you want to generate a report that includes sales and credits by region.

The sales data is at the summary layer.

Region	Total Sales
East	$ 1,000,000
North	$ 120,000
South	$ 3,000,000
West	$ 1,400,000

The credit data is at the detail layer and it is recorded by location.

Region	Location	Total Credits
East	NY	$ 1,500
East	CT	$ 1,800
East	MA	$ 1,600
North	MI	$ 1,400
South	AL	$ 1,900
South	GA	$ 2,000
South	FL	$ 1,900
West	CA	$ 1,200
West	NV	$ 1,600

If you add both of these fields to a report, you will get this:

Region	Total Sales	Location	Total Credits	
East	$ 1,000,000	NY	$ 1,500	Duplicate Data
East	$ 1,000,000	CT	$ 1,800	
East	$ 1,000,000	MA	$ 1,600	
North	$ 120,000	MI	$ 1,400	
South	$ 3,000,000	AL	$ 1,900	
South	$ 3,000,000	GA	$ 2,000	
South	$ 3,000,000	FL	$ 1,900	
West	$ 1,400,000	CA	$ 1,200	
West	$ 1,400,000	NV	$ 1,600	

If you were to summarize the data from this report, your credits would be right but sales would be significantly overstated!

Region	Total Sales	Total Credits
East	$ 3,000,000	$ 4,900
North	$ 120,000	$ 1,400
South	$ 9,000,000	$ 5,800
West	$ 2,800,000	$ 2,800
	$ 14,920,000	$ 14,900

Sales are only $5.5M

To solve this: create two reports, add the same field (Region) to each report, summarize them, and combine them using Excel.

Report 1

Region	Total Sales
East	$ 1,000,000
North	$ 120,000
South	$ 3,000,000
West	$ 1,400,000

Report 2

Region	Location	Total Credits
East	NY	$ 1,500
East	CT	$ 1,800
East	MA	$ 1,600
North	MI	$ 1,400
South	AL	$ 1,900
South	GA	$ 2,000
South	FL	$ 1,900
West	CA	$ 1,200
West	NV	$ 1,600

Summarize both reports: Report 1, Sales is already summarized, so let's summarize Report 2, Credits.

Region	Total Credits	
East	$	4,900
North	$	1,400
South	$	5,800
West	$	2,800
	$	14,900

Combine using Excel (See Chapter 4, Automate in Excel for details). Now the data is correct!

Region	Total Sales		Total Credits	
East	$	1,000,000	$	4,900
North	$	120,000	$	1,400
South	$	3,000,000	$	5,800
West	$	1,400,000	$	2,800
	$	5,520,000	$	14,900

Let's review the examples from Chapter 2, Visualize the Process and Quantify Savings, and discuss the changes we recommended making to the reports.

EXAMPLE 1: SALES AND CREDITS BY LOCATION
We recommended the following changes to the reports:

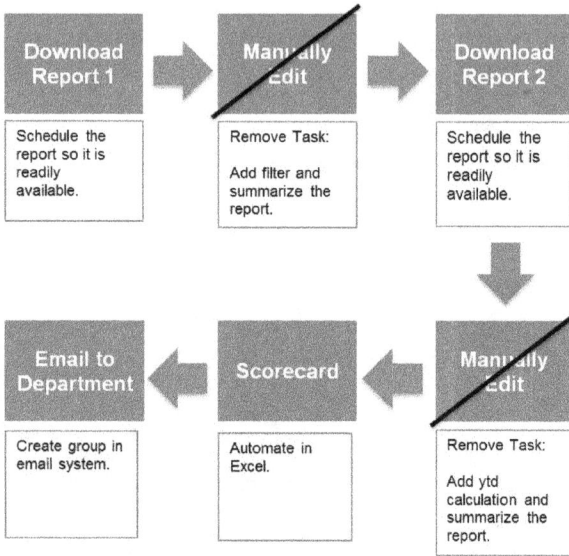

Schedule Reports: You may be able to do this in a few systems, but I usually find that access to scheduling reports is restricted to IT because they can see what else is scheduled to run at the same time. This helps them to manage system availability.

Time: I recommend scheduling reports during the middle of the night so the reports will not slow the system down during normal business hours. The reports will also then be available when you arrive in the morning.

Delivery Method: Reports can be delivered in a few ways:
• Run and save in the system. You will just need to log in and download them.

- Email. I don't recommend this if the file is very large.
- Shared folder
- Intranet site

Add Filter: Add a filter to Report 1 that removes lines where the total = $0 and summarize the report by location.

Adding filters to a report is a quick change that can make the difference between semi and fully automating a report. I always add filters when possible so I don't have to do this manually.

Add Year to Date Field: Add a year to date column to Report 2 and summarize the report by location.

The year to date calculation is either saved in the database or it can be a calculated field on a report. I prefer to add the calculation to the database because the latter alternative can cause an issue that I will describe later. If the field is not recorded in the database, work with IT to see if it can be added as a custom field.

If you are unable to add the field to the database, then you will likely need to include every month on a report and then add a calculated field to the report that summarizes the totals for every month (YTD).

Let's say we are in June and have the following data:

Region	Jan	Feb	Mar	Apr	May	Jun	YTD
East	$ 500	$ 200	$ 300	$ 100	$ 20	$ 800	$ 1,920
North	$ 200	$ 150	$ 700	$ 5	$ 50	$ 100	$ 1,205
South	$ 100	$ 300	$ 100	$ 8	$ 700	$ 200	$ 1,408
West	$ 5	$ 10	$ 15	$ 35	$ 8	$ 4	$ 77
	$ 805	$ 660	$ 1,115	$ 148	$ 778	$ 1,104	$ 4,610

So what happens when July comes around? There are two options:

Non-automated solution: Adjust the report every month to include the current month and adjust the calculation.

or

Automated solution: See if the report will let you add blank columns. I prefer this alternative as I'd prefer not to adjust the reports every month.

Region	Jan	Feb	Mar	Apr	May	Jun	Jul	Aug	Sept	Oct	Nov	Dec	YTD
East	$ 500	$ 200	$ 300	$ 100	$ 20	$ 800							$ 1,920
North	$ 200	$ 150	$ 700	$ 5	$ 50	$ 100							$ 1,205
South	$ 100	$ 300	$ 100	$ 8	$ 700	$ 200							$ 1,408
West	$ 5	$ 10	$ 15	$ 35	$ 8	$ 4							$ 77
	$ 805	$ 660	$ 1,115	$ 148	$ 778	$ 1,104							$ 4,610

Here is the potential issue that I mentioned before:

Region	Jan	Feb	Mar	Apr	May	Jun	Jul	Aug	Sept	Oct	Nov	Dec	YTD
East	$ 500	$ 200	$ 300	$ 100	$ 20	$ 800	#ERROR	#ERROR	#ERROR	#ERROR	#ERROR	#ERROR	#ERROR
North	$ 200	$ 150	$ 700	$ 5	$ 50	$ 100	#ERROR	#ERROR	#ERROR	#ERROR	#ERROR	#ERROR	#ERROR
South	$ 100	$ 300	$ 100	$ 8	$ 700	$ 200	#ERROR	#ERROR	#ERROR	#ERROR	#ERROR	#ERROR	#ERROR
West	$ 5	$ 10	$ 15	$ 35	$ 8	$ 4	#ERROR	#ERROR	#ERROR	#ERROR	#ERROR	#ERROR	#ERROR
	$ 805	$ 660	$ 1,115	$ 148	$ 778	$ 1,104	#ERROR	#ERROR	#ERROR	#ERROR	#ERROR	#ERROR	#ERROR

Please visit www.LetTechnologyDoTheWork.com for full image.

If the system doesn't allow you to display zero values or sum on zero values, then your report errors out. The best solution to this is to record the year to date calculation in the database.

Delivery information: Create a distribution group in the email system that includes everyone in the accounting department.

You can usually create a group in most email systems and add people to a group. This will enable you to select a group when sending an email rather than manually adding people from a list, which could take a while. Adding people manually could also result in sending reports to the wrong users.

Let's review the changes from Example 2.

EXAMPLE 2: SALES BY REGION

We recommended the following changes to the reports:

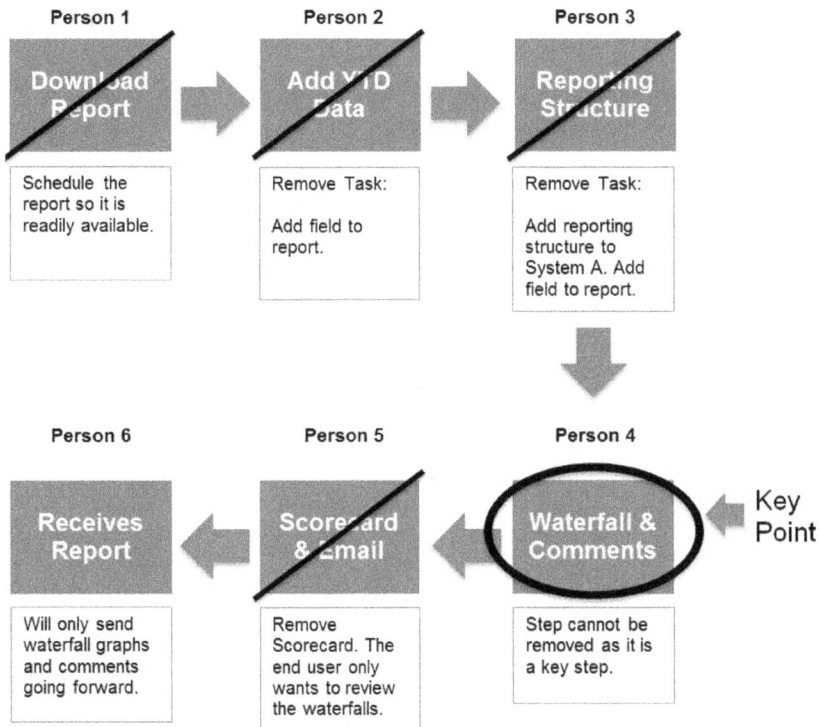

Person 1	Person 2	Person 3
~~Download Report~~	~~Add YTD Data~~	~~Reporting Structure~~
Schedule the report so it is readily available.	Remove Task: Add field to report.	Remove Task: Add reporting structure to System A. Add field to report.

Person 6	Person 5	Person 4	
Receives Report	~~Scorecard & Email~~	Waterfall & Comments	← Key Point
Will only send waterfall graphs and comments going forward.	Remove Scorecard. The end user only wants to review the waterfalls.	Step cannot be removed as it is a key step.	

See *Schedule Reports* and *Add Year to Date Field* in Example 1 for details.

Add Reporting Structure: There are many ways in which companies want to roll the data up and unfortunately this can change frequently. I recommend meeting with stakeholders and trying to define a reporting structure throughout the organization in order to drive consistency in all reporting. For example, if reports are manually manipulated, a location can roll up into one business unit on one report and another business unit in another report. Both of these reports will probably be delivered to the same business owner. This inconsistent roll up causes confusion and rework when analyzing the data. It's better to get everyone on the same page and update the fields in the system so all reports use the same reporting structure.

Not every report can be automated. So what do we do when we have to manually manipulate data for reports? Let's move on to the next chapter to learn how to automate reports in Excel.

NOTES

_____

_____

_____

_____

_____

_____

_____

_____

_____

_____

_____

_____

_____

_____

_____

_____

4
AUTOMATE IN EXCEL

Excel is a very powerful tool that nearly everyone has access to. I have been able to save countless hours by automating in Excel. I set my files up the same way every time so I don't have to reinvent the wheel each time I open a file.

The goal of automating in Excel is to save time AND to increase accuracy. Ideally, we would adjust the reports as described in Chapter 3, Adjust the Reports First. But when we find that we are unable to adjust the reports, we can usually automate the same steps in Excel.

In the following examples, our goal is to combine the data from multiple reports and display a summary in a condensed format. I will walk you through how to set up your files so when you run reports in the future it will only take a few minutes to combine the data. When you are looking to combine reports, find the field that both reports have in common. For Example 1, Region is included in both reports and since we want to display the results by Region, this is the field that we will use. If you are looking at reports and can't find a common field or the field that you need to report on, then find the relationship between the fields on your report and the field that you need. For instance in Example 2, every Location has a Region. You can add the Location field to the report and then create a reference table that maps a Location to a Region. Then, using this relationship, you can add the Region to the report in Excel using the VLOOKUP formula.

Once you select the field or establish the relationship, combining the data is easy. First, summarize the reports if they are not already summarized (see the discussion about layers of data in Chapter 3, Adjust the Reports First). Next, populate the results into a condensed format.

In the following examples, we will use pivot tables to summarize the data and the VLOOKUP formula to populate the results into a scorecard. Let's get started by walking through how to set the file up for the reports in Chapter 2, Visualize the Process and Quantify Savings Example 1.

SETTING THE FILE UP, EXAMPLE 1: SALES AND CREDITS BY LOCATION

One person combines data from two reports, each from a different system, and creates a scorecard. The scorecard shows sales and credits by location.

- Run Report 1, Total Sales, and download it to Excel.

- Report 1. Sort and remove all rows where the total is equal to $0.

- Report 1. Summarize by location.

- Run Report 2, Total Credits, and download it to Excel.

- Report 2. Sort and add a year to date calculation.

- Report 2. Summarize by location.

- Create a scorecard showing results from Report 1 and Report 2.

- Email to department.

You can download sample reports at www.LetTechnologyDoTheWork.com.

1. Download Report 1, Total Sales. Open an Excel file, add the report to a tab and name the tab Sales Report. Save the file as Reporting Example.

	A	B	C	D
1	**Region**	**Customer #**	**Total Sales**	
2	East	1	$ 500,000	
3	East	2	$ 500,000	
4	North	3	$ 40,000	
5	North	4	$ 40,000	
6	North	5	$ 40,000	
7	South	6	$ 100,000	
8	South	7	$ 20,000	
9	South	8	$ 300,000	
10	South	9	$ 800,000	
11	South	10	$ 1,000,000	
12	South	11	$ 780,000	
13	West	12	$ 1,400,000	
14	North	13	$ -	
15	South	14	$ -	

2. Create a simple pivot table

    Pivot tables are incredibly powerful. In general, pivot tables group data, summarize data (Count, Sum, Avg, etc.), and allow you to add calculations (for example, field 1 – field 2). They can also be used to provide a list of unique values, display inconsistencies in data, help you to compare multiple datasets, and much more.

    For these two examples, we will use pivot tables to summarize the reports so we can combine data that is at the same layer (see the discussion about layers of data in Chapter 3, Adjust the Reports First). To get started, highlight the data. There are a few ways to do this but I will describe two.

    Highlight the range of data.

Highlight the entire column (preferred method).

If you only highlight the range of data, then the pivot table will only include this data. What happens when the lines of data increase or decrease? You will need to manually adjust this every time. If you select the entire column instead, then you won't have to manually adjust it every time you run it.

Click on Insert, PivotTable, leave the default options and press OK.

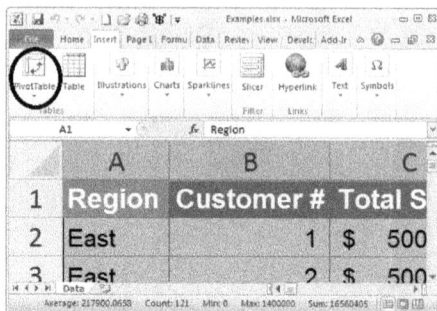

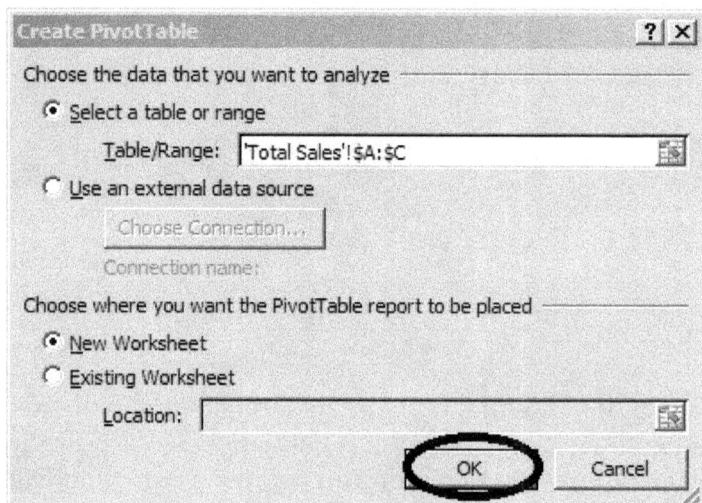

Summarize Report 1 by Region (common field on both reports): Click and drag Region into the Row Labels window and Total Sales into the Values window. Click the down arrow next to Count of Total Sales and select Value Field Settings to change the formula to sum.

Select the Number Format (bottom left corner), adjust the format to currency, set decimals to 0, click OK, and OK again. Rename the tab to Summary Total Sales.

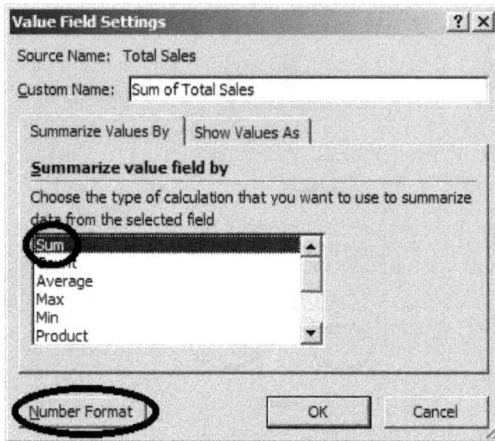

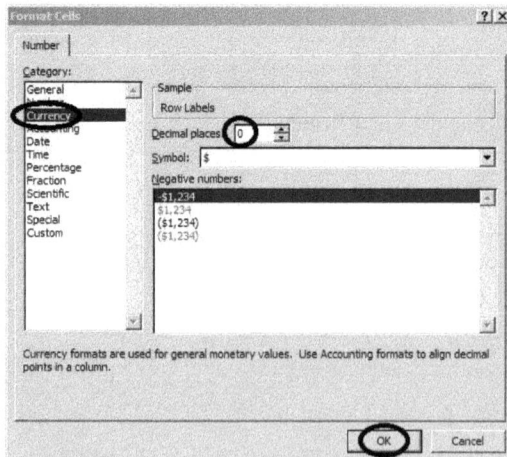

Since you will be including this data in a scorecard and will not be displaying this pivot table, leave the (blank) row in the pivot table. This is a default. If you remove this, then you will need to adjust the filter every time to display new rows. If you leave the (blank), then the pivot table will auto update in the future.

A	B
Row Labels	**Sum of Total Sales**
East	$1,000,000
North	$120,000
South	$3,000,000
West	$1,400,000
(blank)	
Grand Total	**$5,520,000**

3. Summarize Report 2. Download Report 2, Total Credits, and add it to a tab in the Reporting Example workbook. Name the tab Total Credits.

Region	Location	Jan	Feb	Mar	Apr	May
East	NY	700	100	100	500	100
East	CT	900	200	100	100	500
East	MA	500	400	300	100	300
North	MI	100	100	100	600	500
South	AL	200	100	250	300	1,050
South	GA	200	800	800	200	-
South	FL	720	500	300	200	180
West	CA	200	-	300	500	200
West	NV	200	500	400	300	200

Add columns for June thru December and then a YTD column that sums the data for all of the months.

Region	Location	Jan	Feb	Mar	Apr	May	Jun	Jul	Aug	Sep	Oct	Nov	Dec	YTD
East	NY	700	100	100	500	100								1,500
East	CT	900	200	100	100	500								1,800
East	MA	500	400	300	100	300								1,600
North	MI	100	100	100	600	500								1,400
South	AL	200	100	250	300	1,050								1,900
South	GA	200	800	800	200	-								2,000
South	FL	720	500	300	200	180								1,900
West	CA	200	-	300	500	200								1,200
West	NV	200	500	400	300	200								1,600

When adding a calculated field to a report, include all of the columns that you will need for the year, add the calculation to the right of the data set and turn the column grey so the next time that you open the file you will remember to copy and paste the formula to the end of the data set. If you add the calculation in the middle of the data set, you will override it the next time that you copy the data.

Summarize by Region (see pivot table steps from section 2): Add Region to Row Labels and YTD to Values and adjust the format to currency. Name the tab Summary Total Credits.

Row Labels	Sum of YTD
East	$4,900
North	$1,400
South	$5,800
West	$2,800
(blank)	
Grand Total	**$14,900**

4. Create a scorecard to display the summary data from both reports.

   The goal is to create the scorecard once and then for it to update automatically when the pivot tables are updated. The formula that I prefer to use is the VLOOKUP formula.

   This is the structure of the scorecard:

Region	Total Sales	Total Credits
East		
North		
South		
West		

   The VLOOKUP formula is used when you want to find data in another table.

   =VLOOKUP(lookup_value,table_array,col_index_num, [range_lookup])

   You can download the scorecard template or create it on your own. Add the scorecard to the first tab of the Reporting Example file and name the tab YTD Scorecard. Let's start at the intersection of row East and column Total Sales (B2) in the scorecard. The value that we want to return ($1M) is in the pivot table that summarizes Report 1 data (Summary Total Sales tab).

	A	B
1		
2		
3	**Row Labels**	**Sum of Total Sales**
4	East	$1,000,000
5	North	$120,000
6	South	$3,000,000
7	West	$1,400,000
8	(blank)	
9	**Grand Total**	**$5,520,000**

Use the VLOOKUP formula with the following values:

Lookup Value: The look up value (what you are looking for) is the cell containing "East" on the scorecard. Type the beginning of the formula "=VLOOKUP(" and when it prompts you for the lookup value click on the cell A2 on the scorecard tab. Type a comma "," to enter the next parameter.

Table Array: Click on the Summary Total Sales tab and select columns A and B (A:B). The lookup value must always be the first column of the array so the formula knows what it is looking for. I also prefer to include the entire column in the array (A:B compared to A1:B4) so the formula will capture the data as the data set increases without having to adjust the range. Type a comma "," to enter the next parameter.

Column Index: The index represents the number of the column that you want to return. The first column in the array is column 1. For this example, we want to return the value in column 2 (type "2"). Type a comma "," to enter the next parameter.

Range Lookup: False will give you an exact match; True will give you an approximate match. For this example, type "false" since we are looking for an exact match. Close the parenthesis or press enter.

Your formula will look like this: =VLOOKUP(A2,'Summary Total Sales'!A:B,2,FALSE)

Drag the formula down the total sales column to populate the values.

	A	B	C
1	Region	Total Sales	Total Credits
2	East	$1,000,000	
3	North	$120,000	
4	South	$3,000,000	
5	West	$1,400,000	
6	Total	$5,520,000	

Repeat these steps for the total credits column (select the Summary Total Credits tab for the credit data). The formula in cell C2 will be:

=VLOOKUP(A2,'Summary Total Credits'!A:B,2,FALSE)

Add a total row under West that sums the Total Sales column and Total Credits column and format the scorecard to currency or accounting.

Your scorecard will look like this:

	A	B	C
1	Region	Total Sales	Total Credits
2	East	$1,000,000	$4,900
3	North	$120,000	$1,400
4	South	$3,000,000	$5,800
5	West	$1,400,000	$2,800
6	Total	$5,520,000	$14,900

LET'S EXPERIENCE THE AUTOMATION, EXAMPLE 1: SALES AND CREDITS BY LOCATION

Now that the file is properly set up, let's run the next month's data so you can see the benefit of the automation. Download reports 1 (Total Sales June Data) and 2 (Total Credits June Data) for June.

Report 1

Region	Customer #	Total Sales
East	1	$ 500,000
East	2	$ 500,000
North	3	$ 40,000
North	4	$ 40,000
North	5	$ 40,000
South	6	$ 100,000
South	7	$ 20,000
South	8	$ 300,000
South	9	$ 800,000
South	10	$ 1,000,000
South	11	$ 780,000
West	12	$ 1,400,000
East	13	$ 500,000
East	14	$ 500,000
North	15	$ 40,000
North	16	$ 40,000
North	17	$ 40,000
South	18	$ 100,000
South	19	$ 20,000
South	20	$ 300,000
South	21	$ 800,000
South	22	$ 1,000,000
South	23	$ 780,000
West	24	$ 1,400,000

Report 2

Region	Location	Jan	Feb	Mar	Apr	May	Jun
East	NY	700	100	100	500	100	1400
East	CT	900	200	100	100	500	1800
East	MA	500	400	300	100	300	1200
North	MI	100	100	100	600	500	1400
South	AL	200	100	250	300	1,050	500
South	GA	200	800	800	200	-	800
South	FL	720	500	300	200	180	700
West	CA	200	-	300	500	200	200
West	NV	200	500	400	300	200	100

Highlight the columns and copy the data including the headers into the Sales Report and Total Credits tabs in the Reporting Example file. When you paste the data, make sure that you start on the correct column; otherwise, you could write over the calculations that you added to the right of the data set (in grey).

Drag the formula in the grey column to the end of the data (in this example, the calculations already covered the data set so this is not applicable).

Click on the pivot table on the Summary Total Sales tab and select Data and Refresh All. Do the same for the Summary Total Credits tab.

Row Labels	Sum of Total Sales
East	$2,000,000
North	$240,000
South	$6,000,000
West	$2,800,000
(blank)	
Grand Total	**$11,040,000**

Row Labels	Sum of YTD
East	$9,300
North	$2,800
South	$7,800
West	$3,100
(blank)	
Grand Total	**$23,000**

56

And the scorecard automatically refreshed!

	A	B	C
1	**Region**	**Total Sales**	**Total Credits**
2	East	$2,000,000	$9,300
3	North	$240,000	$2,800
4	South	$6,000,000	$7,800
5	West	$2,800,000	$3,100
6	Total	$11,040,000	$23,000

Now that the file is automated, the scorecard will take less than a minute to populate after the reports have been downloaded. Remember to always check your batch totals to ensure that the data is correct (check the total sales in the scorecard to the total sales in the Sales Report). This simple example is easily scalable. I run files with thousands of lines and perform the steps above in less than a minute.

SETTING THE FILE UP, EXAMPLE 2: SALES BY REGION

As a recap, the sales manager requested a report that describes the year over year changes by region. Sales by region is maintained in System A by month. The year to date information is available; however, the report that is being used to combine this data is a month to date report. Even though the company reassigned regions late last year, the systems have not been updated; however, the sales manager would like the updates reflected in the report. The sales manager is not using the scorecard but would like to see a graph that shows the sales trend by month. For this example, you are the only person in the process.

- Download the Sales by Region Report from System A for the month of October.

- Add the data from January – September and a calculation that sums the year to date data in Excel.

- Add a tab in Excel that maps the regions differently because the regions that are included in the system are outdated. All of the reference formulas need to be adjusted in the file.

- Add a chart that shows the sales trend by month

You can download sample reports at www.LetTechnologyDoTheWork.com.

1. Download Report 1, Sales by Region, for the month of October. Open an Excel file, add the report to a tab and rename the tab Sales by Region Oct. Save the file as Reporting Example 2.

Region	Location	Oct
East	NY	700
East	CT	900
East	MA	500
North	MI	100
South	AL	200
South	GA	200
South	FL	720
West	CA	200
West	NV	200

2. Add it to the January – September data. There are many ways to do this, but the way that I would approach it is to add the new month below the old months.

Open the Sales by Region Jan-Sep file. Add the data to a tab in the Reporting Example 2 workbook and name the tab History Data. Next, copy the location and amount columns from the October tab excluding the headers and the regions (we will address the regions later) and paste it below the September data. Type Oct in the month field to reflect the current month.

Location	Amount	Month
NY	1400	Jan
CT	1800	Jan
MA	1000	Jan
MI	200	Jan
AL	400	Jan
GA	400	Jan
FL	1440	Jan
CA	400	Jan
NV	400	Jan
NY	200	Feb
CT	400	Feb
MA	800	Feb
MI	200	Feb
AL	200	Feb
GA	1600	Feb
FL	1000	Feb
CA	0	Feb
NV	1000	Feb
NY	200	Mar
CT	200	Mar
MA	600	Mar

This is the appended October data:

NY	200	Sept
CT	1000	Sept
MA	600	Sept
MI	1000	Sept
AL	2100	Sept
GA	0	Sept
FL	360	Sept
CA	400	Sept
NV	400	Sept
NY	700	Oct
CT	900	Oct
MA	500	Oct
MI	100	Oct
AL	200	Oct
GA	200	Oct
FL	720	Oct
CA	200	Oct
NV	200	Oct

3. Add a table that maps the new regions by location. Open the Region file and copy/paste it into a tab in the Reporting Example 2 workbook and name the tab Region.

Location	Region
NY	East
CT	North
MA	North
MI	Central
AL	South East
GA	South East
FL	South
CA	West
NV	Central

Using the VLOOKUP formula discussed in Example 1, add the regions on the Regions tab to the January – October data on the History Data tab column D. Format the column to grey to signal that there is a formula that needs to be accounted for in the future and name the column Region.

	A	B	C	D
1	Location	Amount	Month	Region
2	NY	1400	Jan	East
3	CT	1800	Jan	North
4	MA	1000	Jan	North
5	MI	200	Jan	Central
6	AL	400	Jan	South East
7	GA	400	Jan	South East
8	FL	1440	Jan	South
9	CA	400	Jan	West
10	NV	400	Jan	Central
11	NY	200	Feb	East
12	CT	400	Feb	North

Your formula in D2 will look like this:
=VLOOKUP(A2,Region!A:B,2,FALSE)

Copy and Paste the VLOOKUP formula to the end of the data set.

4. Create a pivot table based on the History Data tab (see steps in Example 1), name the tab Summary and drag it to the front of the workbook. Add Region to Row Labels, Month to Column Labels and Amount to Values. Change the Amount to Sum and format.

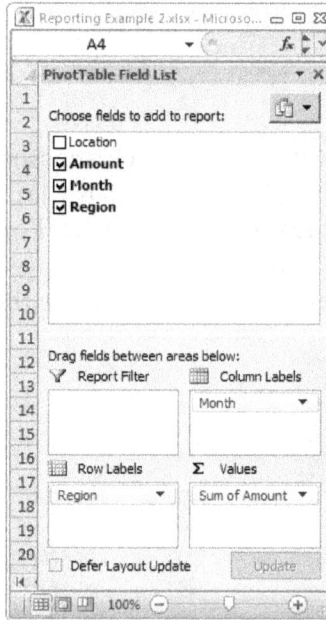

Change the Grand Total Label to YTD (Click in the field that displays Grand Total and type in "YTD").

Please visit www.LetTechnologyDoTheWork.com for full image.

If your columns are not in order by month (see June, July, Sept and Oct), change the order of your pivot table by clicking on June and dragging the box around June in front of July. This will move the entire column. Repeat for September and October.

Please visit www.LetTechnologyDoTheWork.com for full image.

5. To create a chart, highlight the entire pivot table. Include the filters if you have filters on your pivot table. Click Insert, and then select Line and the first 2-D line option.

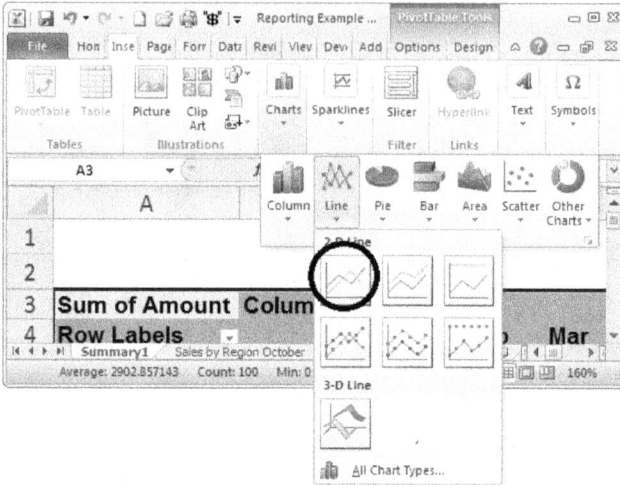

The (blank) will be included in the chart if you do not filter it out. Click on the arrows next to the row and column labels on your pivot table and deselect (blank). Now that you have deselected (blank), you will need to check this filter every time you run the file to ensure that you do not exclude a month or a region.

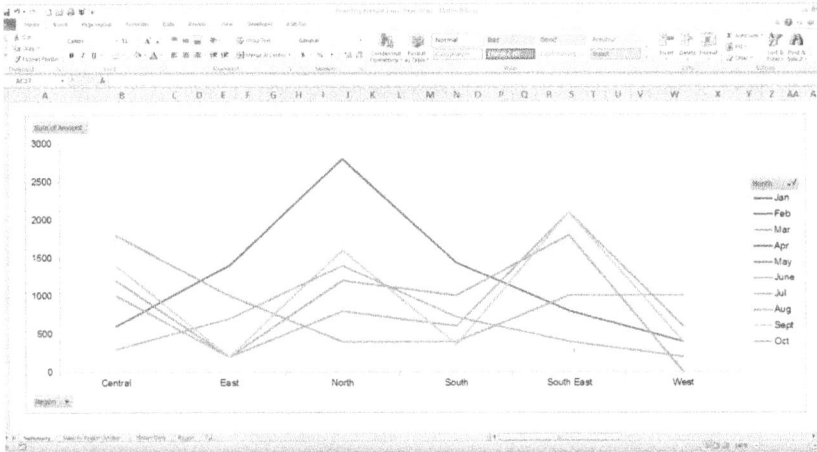

The axis on this chart needs to be flipped so the months are across the bottom.

Right click on the chart and click Select Data.

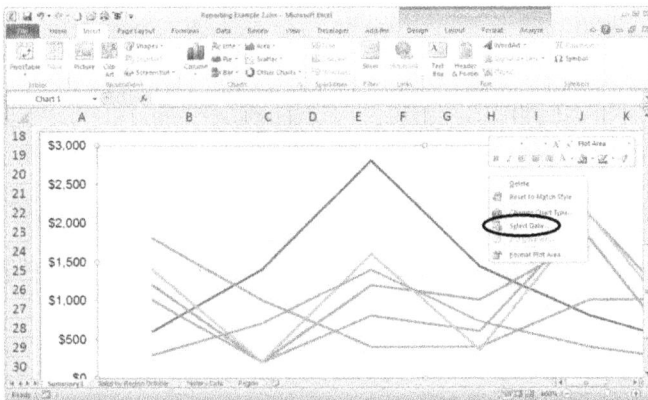

Click the Switch Row/Column button and click OK.

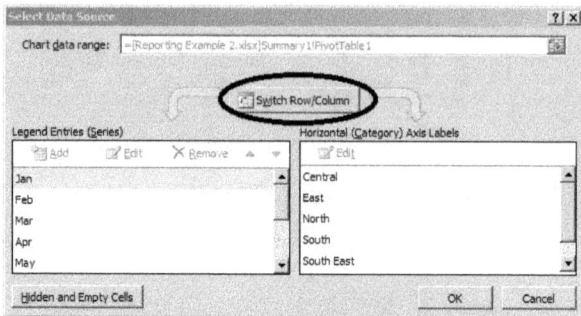

Right click on the Sum of Amount label on the chart and select the Hide All Field Buttons on Chart.

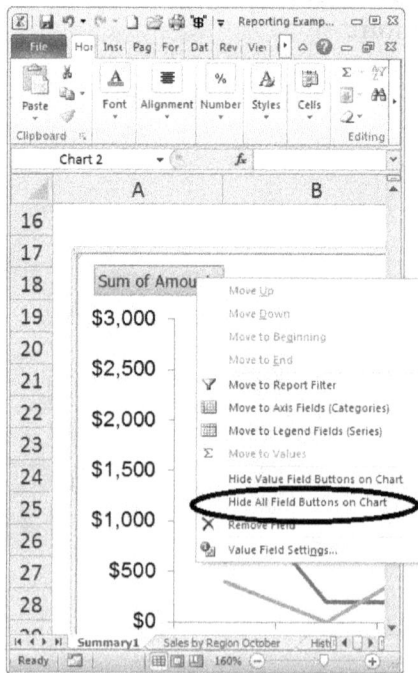

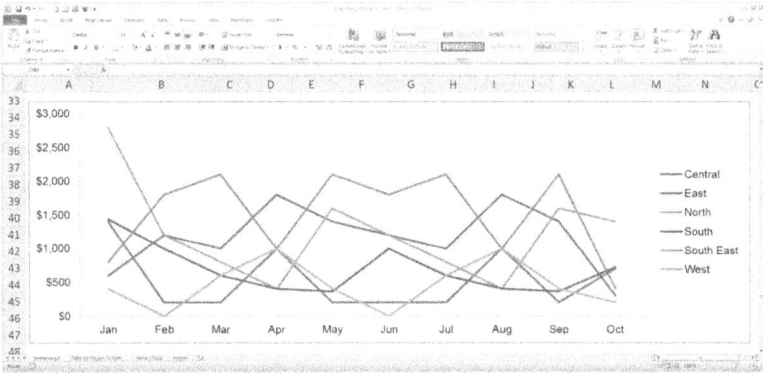

LET'S EXPERIENCE THE AUTOMATION, EXAMPLE 2: SALES BY REGION

Now that the file is properly set up, let's run the next month's data so you can see the benefit of the automation. Download the Sales by Region Report for November and save it over the Sales by Region Oct tab or as its own tab in the Reporting Example 2 workbook.

Region	Location	Nov
East	NY	1200
East	CT	1800
East	MA	2400
North	MI	400
South	AL	2
South	GA	0
South	FL	800
West	AR	12
West	NV	150

Copy and Paste the November data below the October data on the History Data tab. Remember to only copy the location and value and exclude the headers and regions. Add "Nov" to the blank cells and then copy/paste (or drag) the formula in grey to the end of the data set.

If you are missing a value in your reference table (the Region tab in this example), you will receive an N/A. Add the data to the reference table (Region tab) and the data will populate. For this example, AR is not defined on the Region tab. Click on the Region tab and add "AR" to the bottom of the table and assign it to the Central region.

Data set is missing a reference:

	A	B	C	D
95	MI	400	Nov	Central
96	AL	2	Nov	South East
97	GA	0	Nov	South East
98	FL	800	Nov	South
99	AR	12	Nov	#N/A
100	NV	150	Nov	Central

Add the reference in the Region tab.

Location	Region
NY	East
CT	North
MA	North
MI	Central
AL	South East
GA	South East
FL	South
CA	West
NV	Central
AR	Central

The History Data tab will automatically update:

	A	B	C	D
95	MI	400	Nov	Central
96	AL	2	Nov	South East
97	GA	0	Nov	South East
98	FL	800	Nov	South
99	AR	12	Nov	Central
100	NV	150	Nov	Central

Click on your pivot table on the Summary tab, refresh (Data, Refresh All) and adjust the month filter. Click on the arrow next to Row Labels to add Nov (this is the result of filtering the blank row). Now the chart will automatically update.

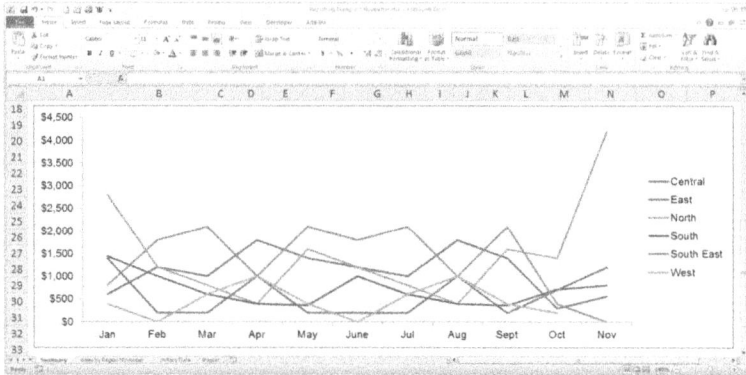

That's it! This file will take us under 5 minutes to run.

These are simple reporting examples that are easily scalable. Focus on setting your files up consistently every time so all you have to do is repopulate the data and all of the summary information will automatically update. Next, let's review how to add two data sets together and how to find inconsistencies in data sets.

BONUS TIP 1

If you need to add two data sets together that are in the same order, highlight the area that you want to add, copy it and "add" it. See the steps below:

1. Highlight the area that you want to add

2. Copy it.

3. Highlight the area that you want to add the data to.

	A	B	C	D	E	F	G	H	I	J	K
1	Location	Jan	Feb	Mar	Apr	May	June	Jul	Aug	Sept	Oct
2	NY	700	100	100	500	100	100	100	500	100	700
3	CT	900	200	100	100	500	200	100	100	500	900
4	MA	500	400	300	100	300	400	300	100	300	500
5	MI	100	100	100	600	500	100	100	600	500	100
6	AL	200	100	250	300	1050	100	250	300	1050	200
7	GA	200	800	800	200	0	800	800	200	0	200
8	FL	720	500	300	200	180	500	300	200	180	720
9	CA	200	0	300	500	200	0	300	500	200	200
10	NV	200	500	400	300	200	500	400	300	200	200
11	NY	700	100	100	500	100	100	100	500	100	700
12	CT	900	200	100	100	500	200	100	100	500	900
13	MA	500	400	300	100	300	400	300	100	300	500
14	MI	100	100	100	600	500	100	100	600	500	100
15	AL	200	100	250	300	1050	100	250	300	1050	200
16	GA	200	800	800	200	0	800	800	200	0	200
17	FL	720	500	300	200	180	500	300	200	180	720
18	CA	200	0	300	500	200	0	300	500	200	200
19	NV	200	500	400	300	200	500	400	300	200	200

4. Right click and Paste Special.

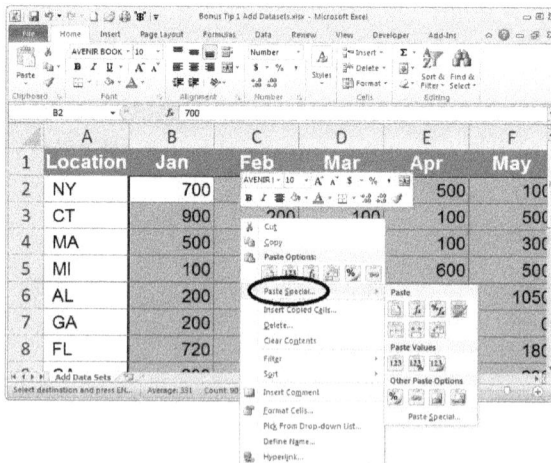

5. Select Add and OK (you can also subtract, multiple and divide).

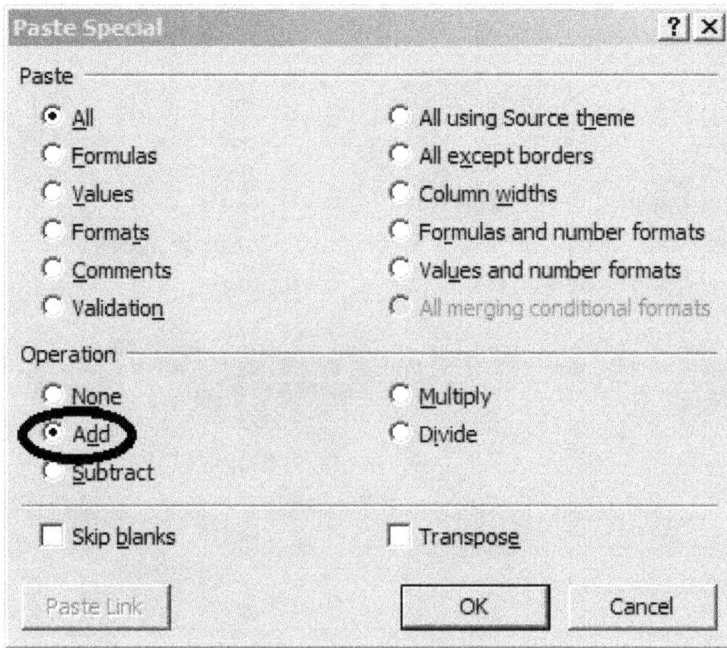

6. Remove the data that you added (data in step 1).

BONUS TIP 2

To find the variances in data sets, add the source in a column, stack the data sets, create a pivot table, and review the counts. For example, the following two reports should include the same data but, after comparing the counts, I noticed that the report from System A includes California but the report from System B does not. Download the data from System A. Open an Excel file, copy and paste the System A data into a tab and name the tab System A. Save the file as Bonus 2 Reporting Example.

Location	Amount
MA	1,200
FL	1,300
GA	14,000
NY	15,000
CA	16,000

Download the data from System B, copy and paste the data into a new tab in the Bonus 2 Reporting Example workbook, and name the tab System B.

Location	Amount
MA	1,200
FL	1,300
GA	14,000
NY	15,000

On the System A tab, insert a column (A), name it Source and add System A to the Source column.

	A	B	C
1	Source	Location	Amount
2	System A	MA	1,200
3	System A	FL	1,300
4	System A	GA	14,000
5	System A	NY	15,000
6	System A	CA	16,000

On the System B tab, insert a column (A), name it Source and add System B to the Source column.

	A	B	C
1	**Source**	**Location**	**Amount**
2	System B	MA	1,200
3	System B	FL	1,300
4	System B	GA	14,000
5	System B	NY	15,000

Stack the data sets together on a new tab and name the tab Combined.

	A	B	C
1	**Source**	**Location**	**Amount**
2	System A	MA	1,200
3	System A	FL	1,300
4	System A	GA	14,000
5	System A	NY	15,000
6	System A	CA	16,000
7	System B	MA	1,200
8	System B	FL	1,300
9	System B	GA	14,000
10	System B	NY	15,000

Create a pivot table, name the tab Summary, select the Location as the Row Label, Source as the Column Label and Source as the Value. We will count on the Source because we are trying to determine how many times each value appears in each source system. If the data is in every source, the grand total will equal the number of source files.

	A	B	C	D	E
3	**Count of Source**	**Column Labels**			
4	**Row Labels**	**System A**	**System B**	**(blank)**	**Grand Total**
5	CA	1			1
6	FL	1	1		2
7	GA	1	1		2
8	MA	1	1		2
9	NY	1	1		2
10	(blank)				
11	**Grand Total**	5	4		9

In this example, the grand total will be 2 if the location is included in both reports. The only grand total that is not 2 is CA, so you know CA is the issue. The columns indicate which reports include the location. In this example, since System B is blank then CA is not included in System B.

Visit my website at www.lettechnologydothework.com for more complex examples and advanced tips.

Now that we've learned how to automate in Excel, let's move on to Chapter 5 to learn how to automate in Access.

NOTES

5

AUTOMATE IN ACCESS

I prefer to use Access to automate files if a report is more complex, contains a lot of data, requires a lot of changes, or has several inputs. You can either use the query wizard or write SQL statements, whichever is easier for you. In this chapter, we'll walk through how to create tables, queries, and a form for easy input. There is so much that Access can do but I only touch on a few tips below. Let's continue with Example 1 from Chapter 4, Automate in Excel.

SETTING THE FILE UP, EXAMPLE 1: SALES AND CREDITS BY LOCATION

One person combines data from two reports, each from a different system, and creates a scorecard. The scorecard shows sales and credits by location.

- Run Report 1, Total Sales, and download it to Excel.

- Report 1. Sort and remove all rows where the total is equal to $0.

- Report 1. Summarize by location.

- Run Report 2, Total Credits, and download it to Excel.

- Report 2. Sort and add a year to date calculation.

- Report 2. Summarize by location.

- Create a scorecard showing results from Report 1 and Report 2.

- Email to department.

You can download sample reports at www.LetTechnologyDoTheWork.com.

1. To create the database, open Access, click on Blank database, click on the folder next to the file name to select a location, rename the file to Reporting Example, then click on Create.

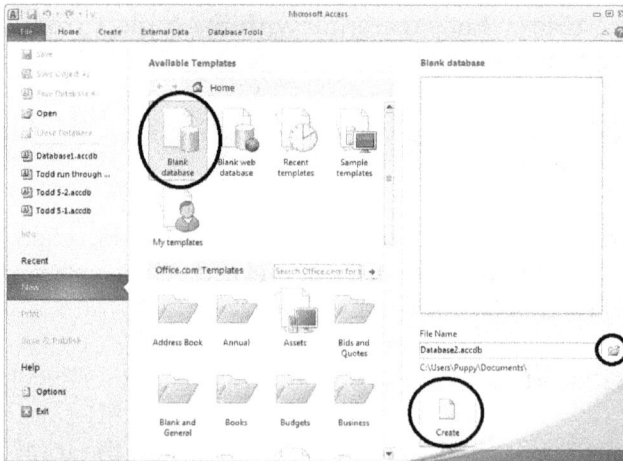

You will see this default table.

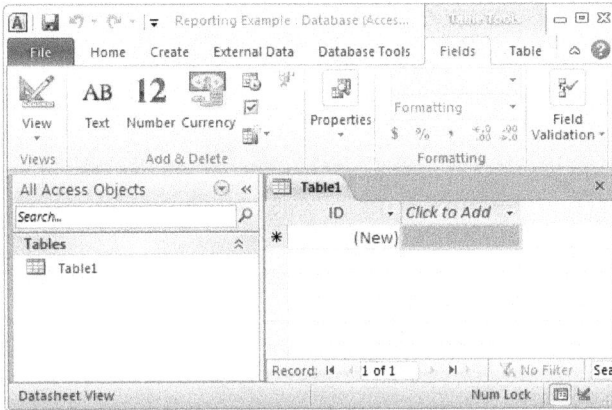

2. Let's create our first table that includes data from Report 1, Total Sales. Always download the reports into Excel. Copy the range of data including the headers.

On the left hand side you will see Table1, the default table. Right click under Table1 and select Paste.

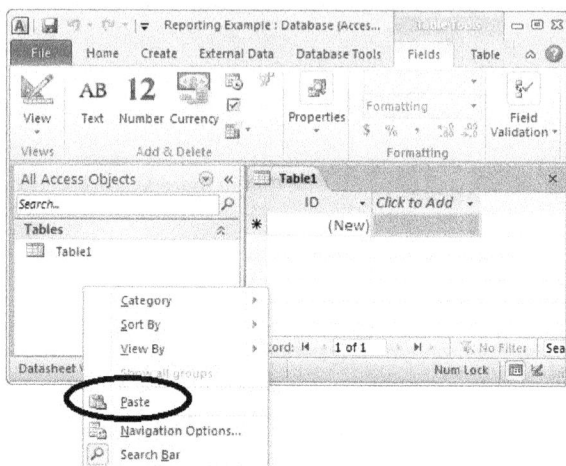

Select Yes when prompted about column headings.

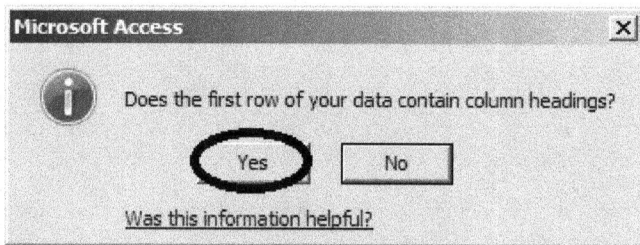

You will receive a confirmation message. Press OK.

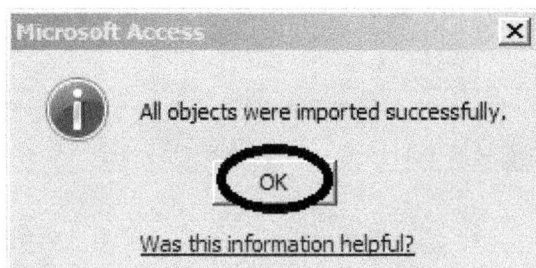

Now your table has been created and will appear under the table area. Right click on the table that you created and rename it to tblTotalSales (no spaces). Include "tbl" before table names, "qry" before query names and "frm" before form names. This will help you to sort and select objects in the future. You can close the default Table1 by clicking on the X in the top right corner, it will automatically be removed from the table list.

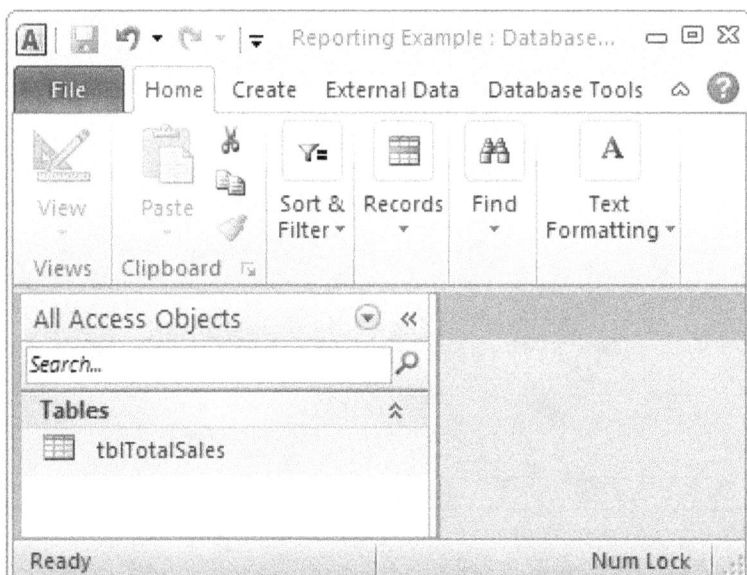

Right click on the table name and select Design View; define the data type for each field.

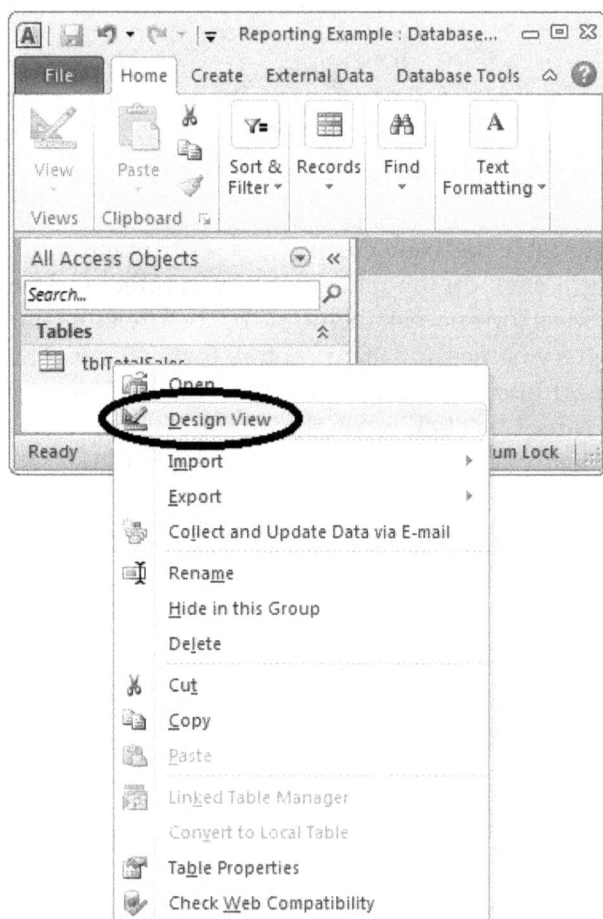

tblTotalSales

Field Name	Data Type
Region	Text
Customer #	Number
Total Sales	Number

Access will usually default the data type to the format set in Excel, but it is always a good idea to verify this. For example, if you create a number and define it as a text field to preserve the leading zeros, you will be unable to add it to a number that is defined as a number. For the field Total Sales, select the Data Type Currency and change the Decimal Places to 0.

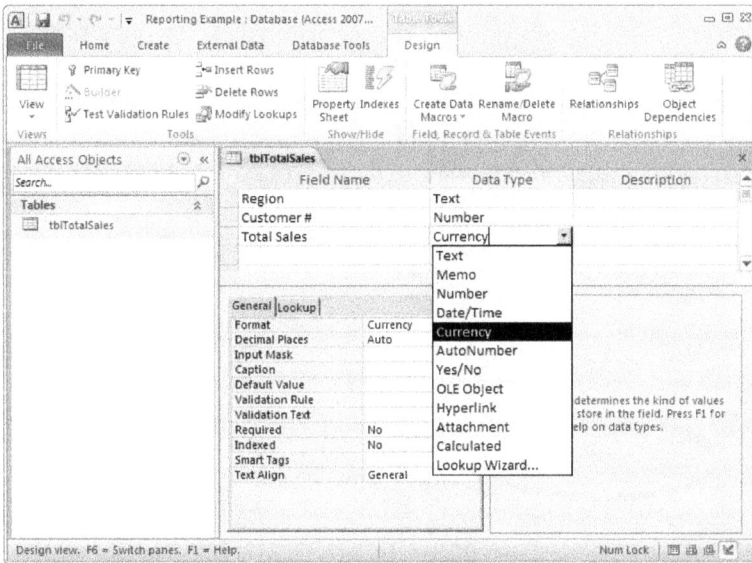

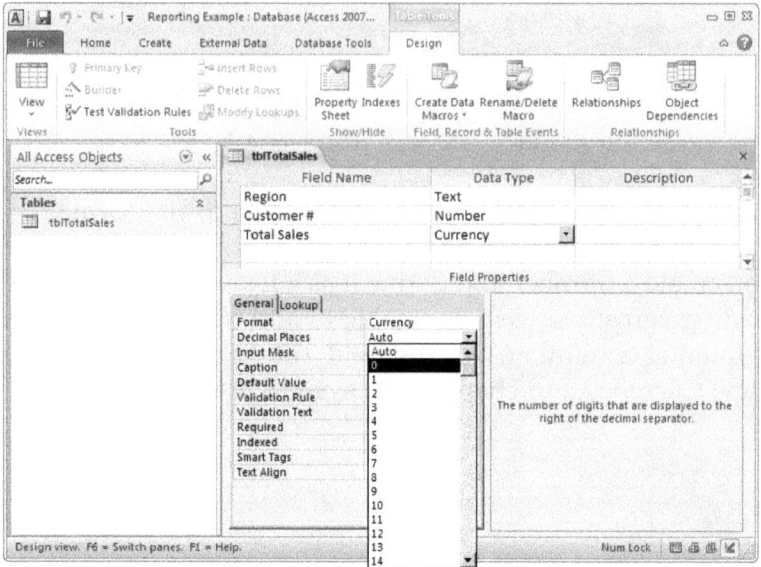

Click on View, Datasheet View to see your table. Save the table when prompted.

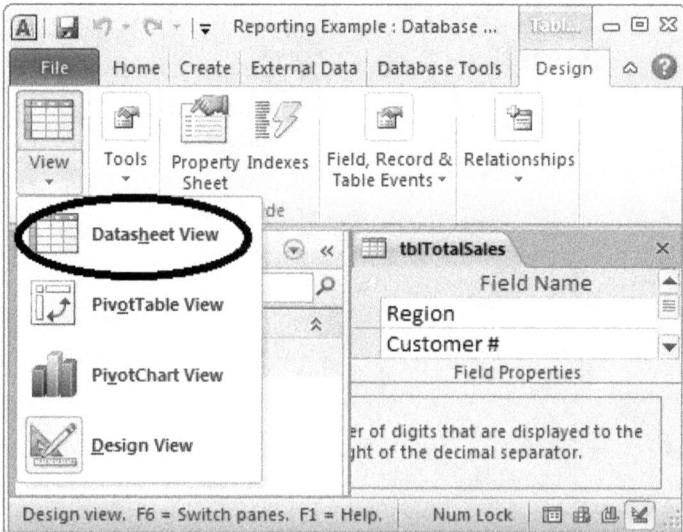

3. To remove all customers with $0 Total Sales, write the following query: Create, then Query Design, then click Close. I prefer to drag and drop the tables rather than select them from this screen.

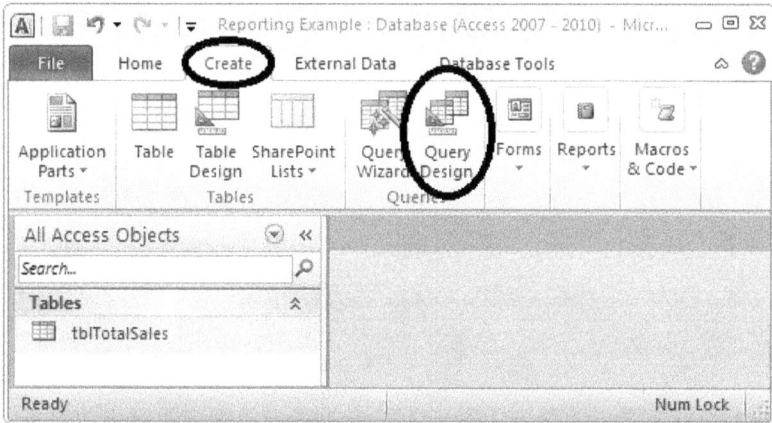

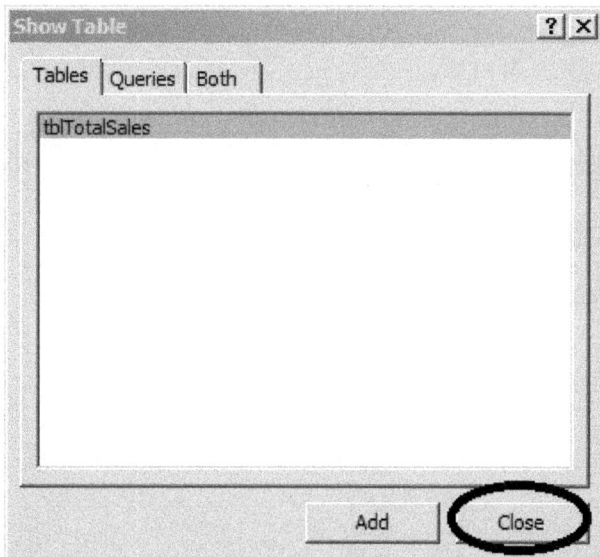

Drag the table tblTotalSales to the query and you will see the field names included in the table.

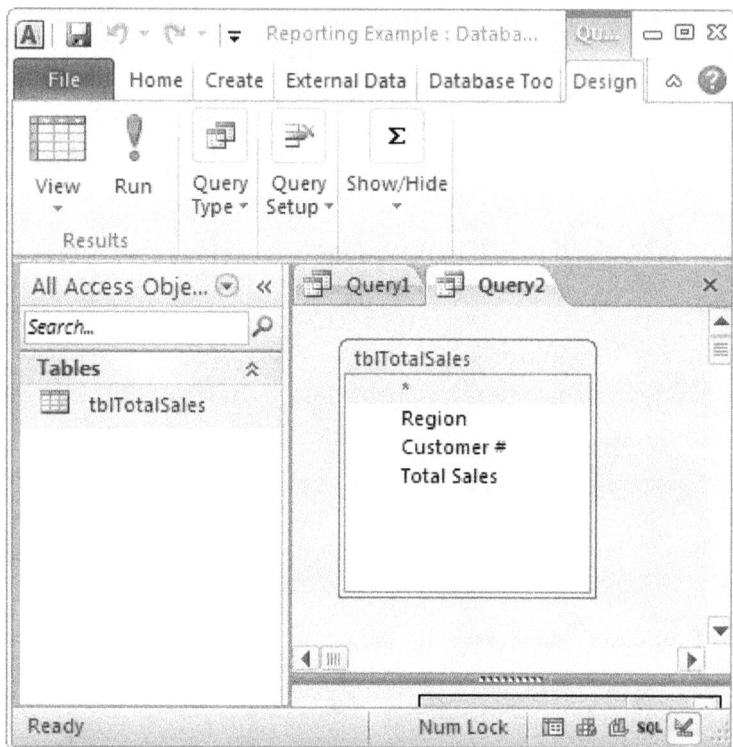

Double click on each of the 3 field names to add them to the bottom section (design grid) and add >0 in the criteria for Total Sales. This will filter out all customers that have Total Sales less than or equal to 0.

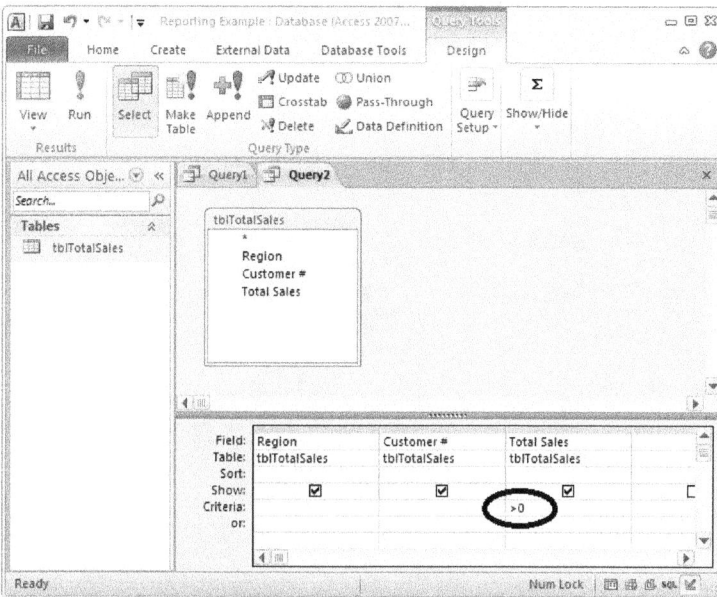

Click Run in the tool bar to see your results (Customers #13 and #14 are excluded because they have $0 Total Sales).

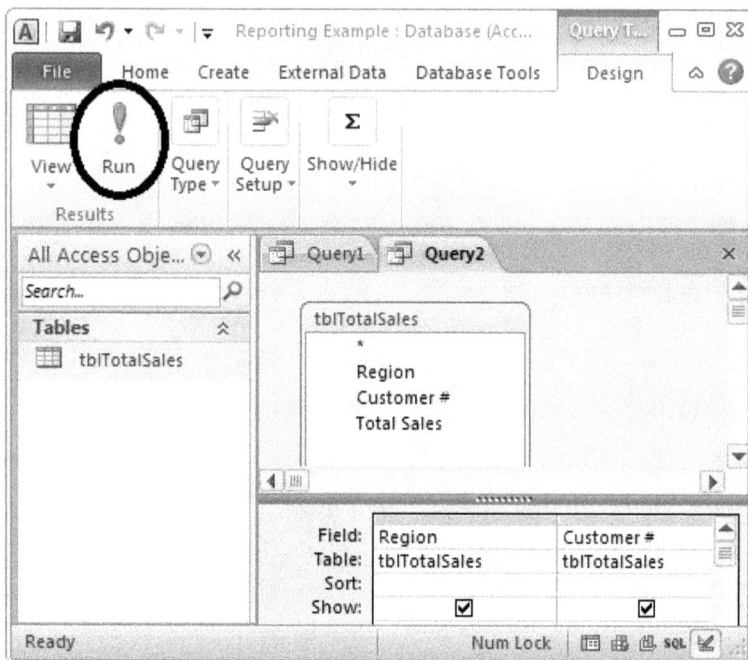

Save and name the query as qryTotalSales_GreaterThanZero.

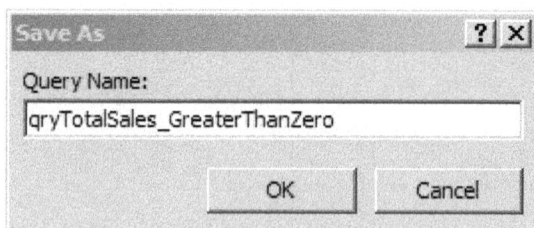

4. To summarize by Region, create a new query (Create, then Query Design, then click Close).

    Add qryTotalSales_GreaterThanZero to the query (drag and drop) and double click on the Region and Total Sales fields. Only select these fields because you want to group Total Sales by Region, not taking into account customer number.

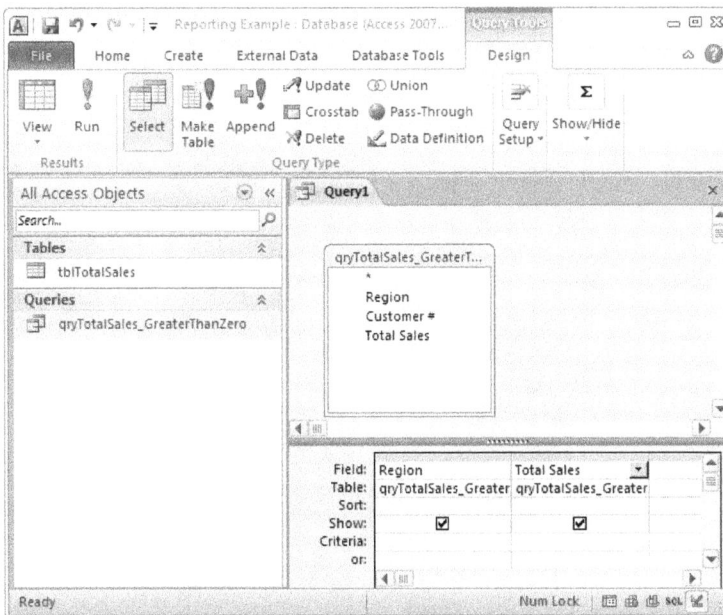

Select the Totals icon on the ribbon to display the Total filter in the design grid of the query.

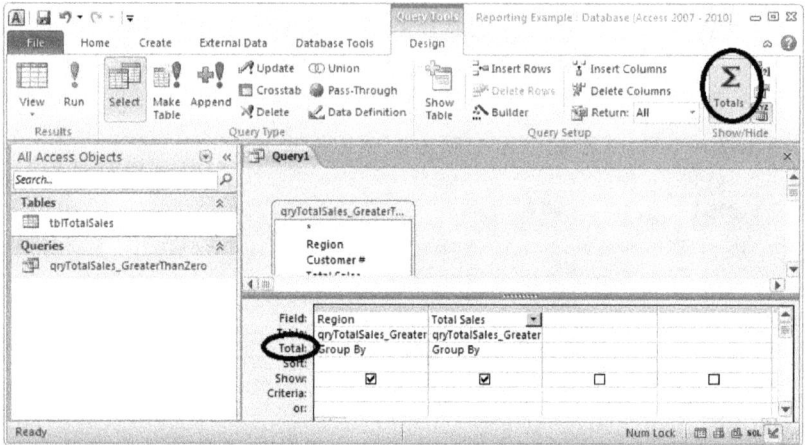

The following options for your query are available (Sum, Avg, Min, etc). For this example, since we are looking to summarize results, select Sum for the Total Sales field. Then select Group By for Region since we want to group by region.

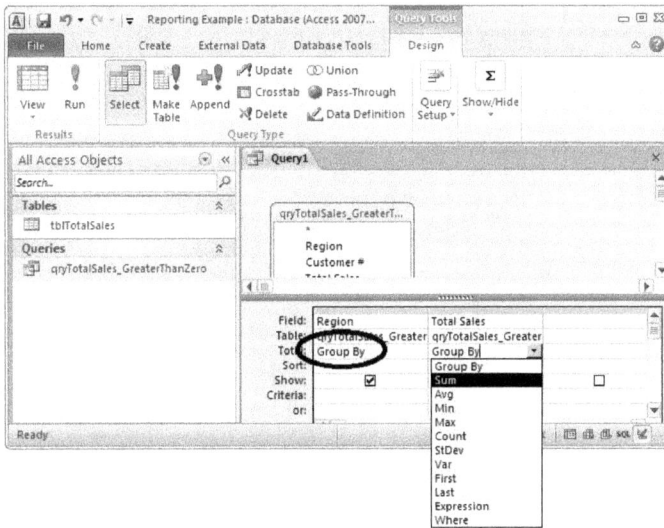

If the Property Sheet is not automatically displayed, you can activate it on the ribbon.

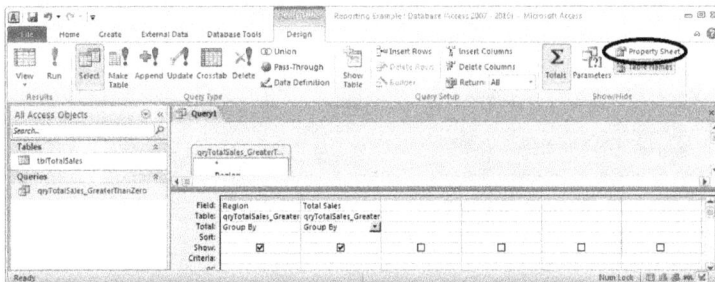

To format Total Sales, click on the Total Sales field, and then select Currency in the Format field and set the Decimal Places to 0 on the Property Sheet.

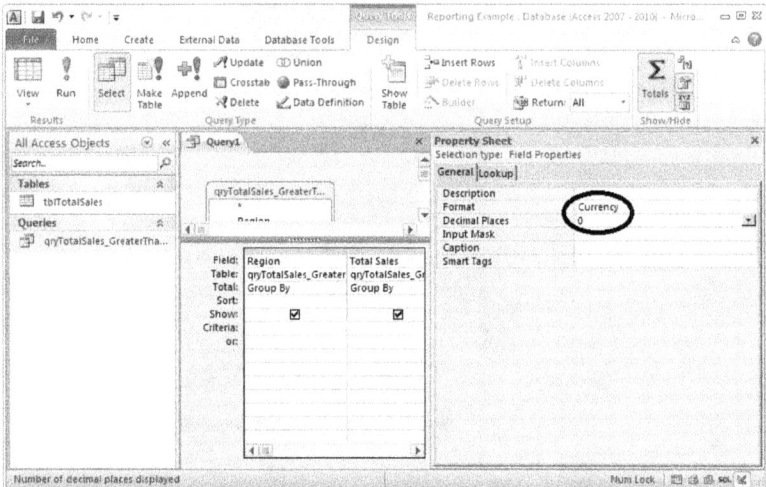

Click on Run and you will see the summary below.

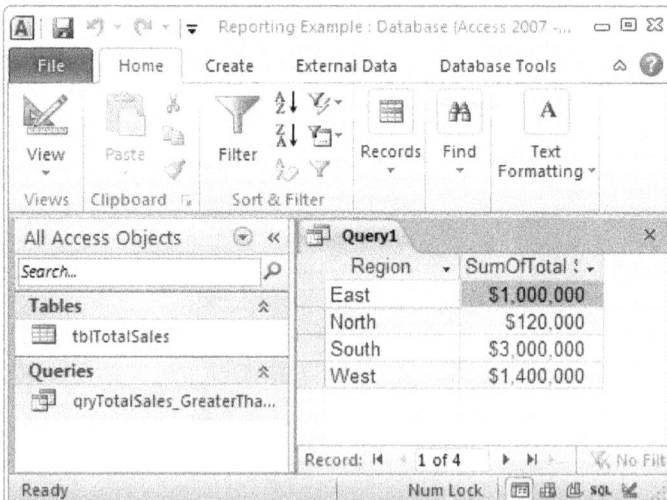

One feature that I find helpful when verifying data is to add a total field to the query in the Data Sheet View. To add a total to the query, click on the totals icon in the toolbar and it will display "Total" under the data. Then click on the cell next to "Total" and select Sum. Save the query as qrySummaryTotalSales.

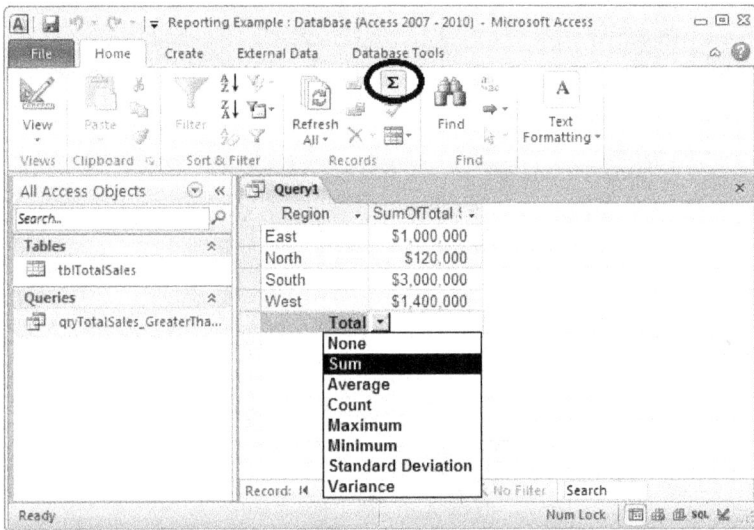

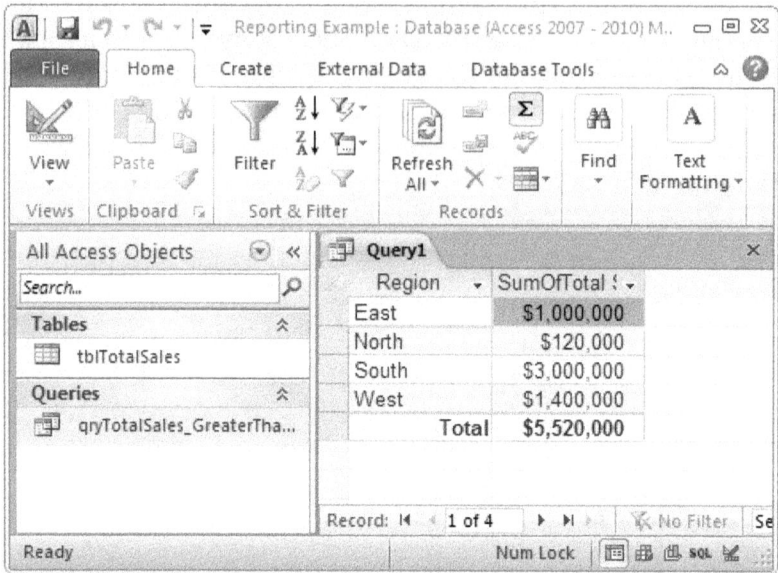

5. Download Report 2, Total Credits, and follow Step 2 for creating a table. Rename the table as tblTotalCredits.

	A	B	C	D	E	F	G
1	Region	Location	Jan	Feb	Mar	Apr	May
2	East	NY	700	100	100	500	100
3	East	CT	900	200	100	100	500
4	East	MA	500	400	300	100	300
5	North	MI	100	100	100	600	500
6	South	AL	200	100	250	300	1,050
7	South	GA	200	800	800	200	0
8	South	FL	720	500	300	200	180
9	West	CA	200	0	300	500	200
10	West	NV	200	500	400	300	200

Since the columns in the report do not include all 12 months, add the additional months to the table using the Design View. As a reminder, select the name of the table (tblTotalCredits), right click, then select Design View. Ensure that these new fields are the same data type as the existing fields. Save and close the table.

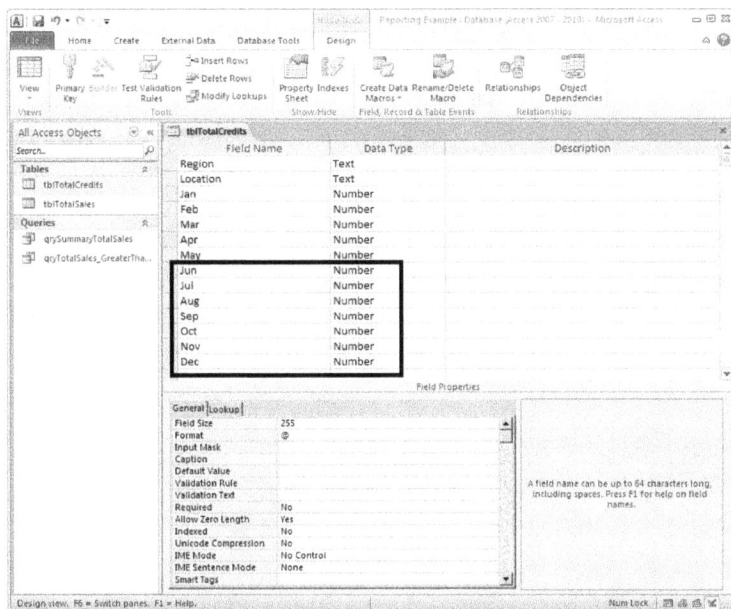

6. To add a Year to Date field, create a query (Create, then Query Design, then click Close) and drag the tblTotalCredits table into the query and include all of the fields except for the * in the bottom box (the design grid). In the next available column, type this formula in the Field:

YTD: NZ([Jan])+NZ([Feb])+ NZ([Mar])+NZ([Apr]) +NZ([May])+NZ([Jun])+NZ([Jul])+NZ([Aug])+NZ([Sep]) +NZ([Oct])+ NZ([Nov])+NZ([Dec])

To rename a field, add the new name and then a colon (:). If you have a field name with a space, add brackets around the field [field name], otherwise you can just include the field name. I used brackets for this example, but since my field names do not have spaces I could exclude the brackets.

The NZ that is before the months on the calculation allows you to add fields that are blank. In this example, June – December are blank so we need the NZ function. If you do not have blank fields, then you do not need the NZ function. But if you have blank fields and you do not include NZ, then you will end up with a blank total.

Click on the field that you would like to add the calculation to and select Shift+F2. This will bring up the expression builder which makes it much easier to build and see the equations.

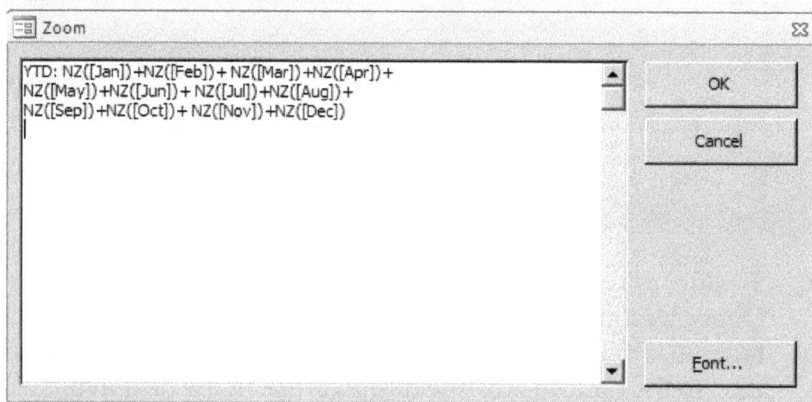

Click on Run and you will see the following query that includes the YTD field. Save the query as qryTotalCreditsYTD.

Please visit www.LetTechnologyDoTheWork.com for full image.

7. To summarize by Region, create a query (Create, then Query Design, then click Close) and add the qryTotalCreditsYTD query. Add the Region and YTD fields to the design grid and select the Totals button on the ribbon. Next, Group By Region and Sum by YTD in the Total row. Save and run the query as qrySummaryTotalCreditsYTD.

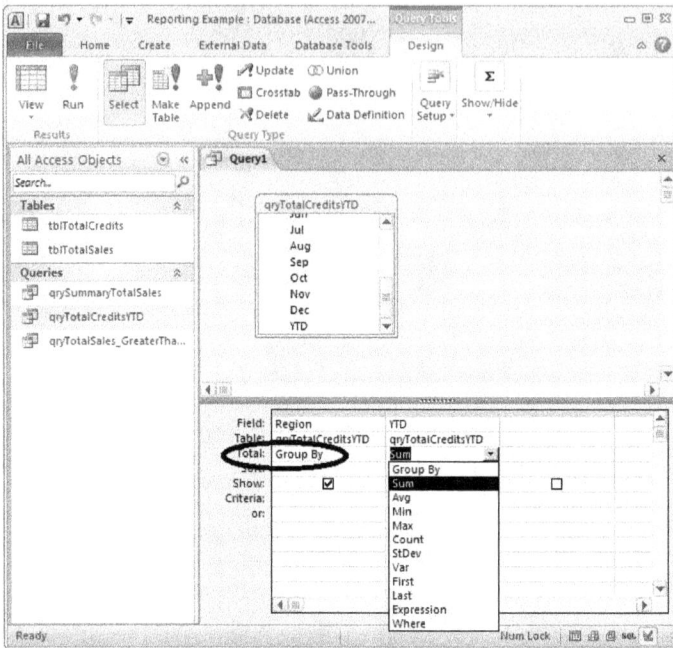

To add a total to the query, click on the Totals icon in the toolbar and it will display "Total" under the data. Then click on the cell next to "Total" and select Sum.

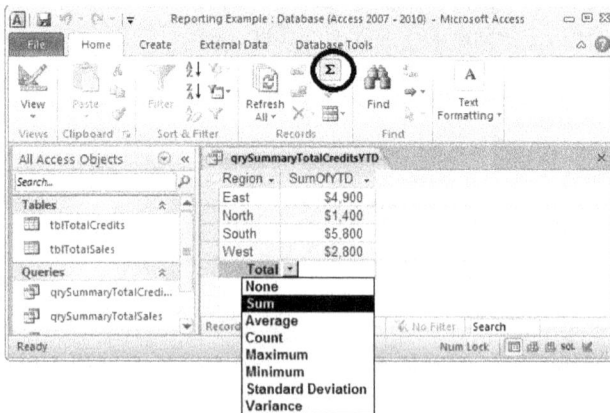

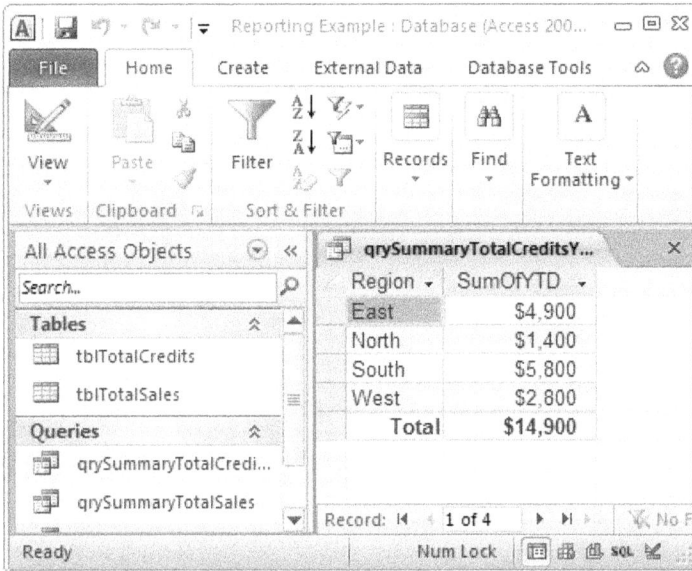

8. Create the Scorecard. Create a new query (Create, then Query Design, then click Close).

   Drag and drop both summary queries (qrySummaryTotalSales and qrySummaryTotalCreditsYTD) to the query.

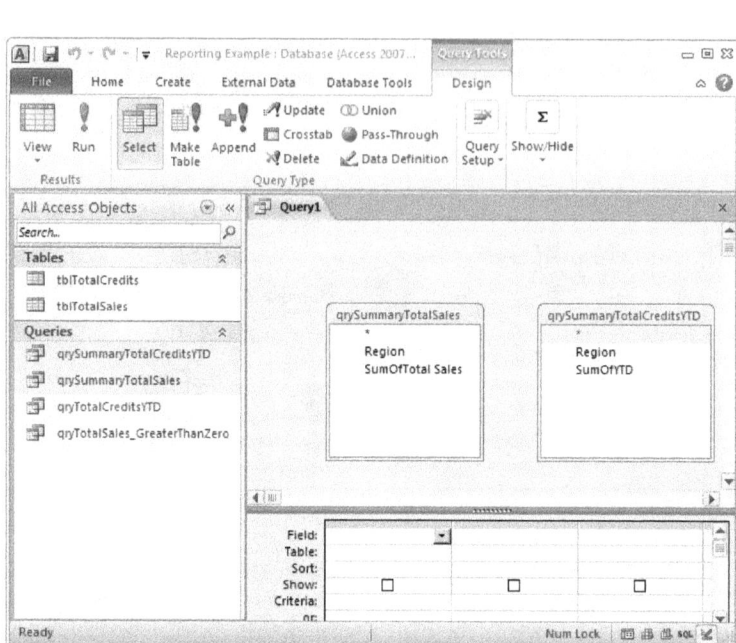

There are three ways to combine data from tables:

1. Data that is included in both tables.
2. All of the data from table 1 and only data from table 2 that matches.
3. All of the data from table 2 and only data from table 1 that matches.

All three options are very important and can cause critical errors if not used correctly. For now, we will use option 2 because the sales table includes all regions.

Click on Region from qrySummaryTotalSales and then drag your curser to Region on qrySummaryTotalCreditsYTD. This will create a join (a line).

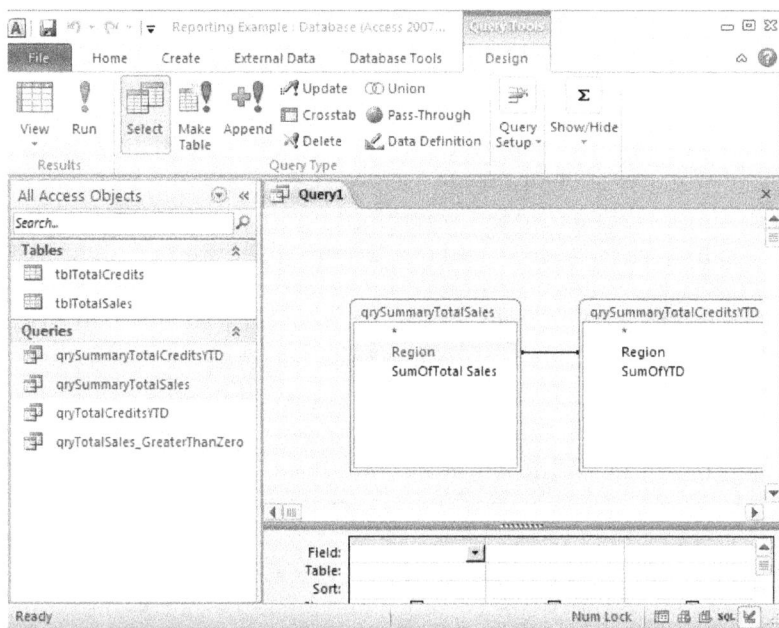

Then double click on the line and select option 2.

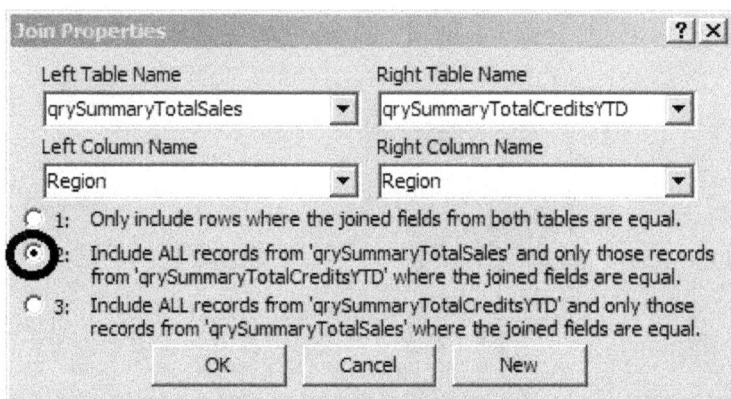

Add the Region and SumOfTotalSales fields from qrySummaryTotalSales and the SumOfYTD field from qrySummary TotalCreditsYTD to the design grid.

Now, let's rename the fields on the query for clarity sake. The original name (field name) must remain the same but you can add a new label to the left separated by a colon (:). For example, new name: field name. Add the label Total Sales to SumOfTotal Sales (Total Sales: SumOfTotal Sales) and YTD Credits to SumOfYTD (YTD Credits: SumOfYTD). Format the columns to currency and set the decimals to 0 (in the Property Sheet).

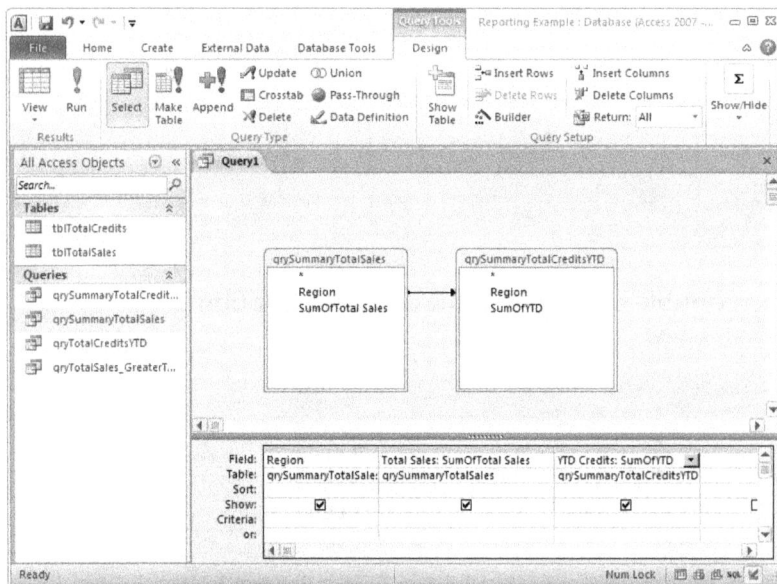

Run the query and add the totals to the scorecard (click the Totals icon and then change the cells to sum). Save the query and name it qryScorecard.

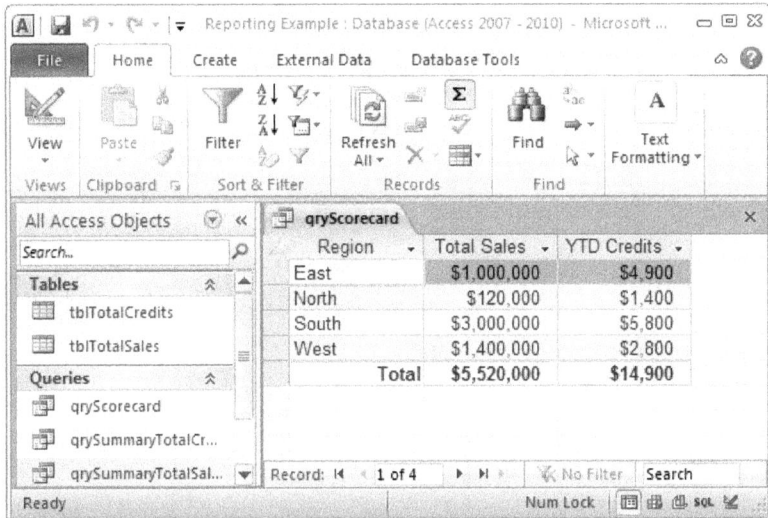

9. Next, let's look at creating a form. Select Create and then Blank Form.

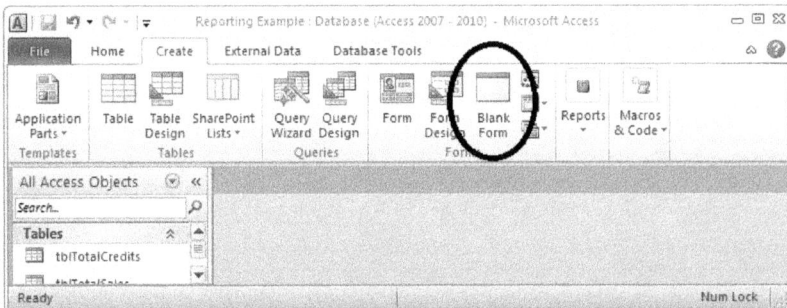

We will add a few buttons to this form to make importing and exporting a breeze. We will need two import buttons, one for each report and an export button for the scorecard.

Click on View, Design View.

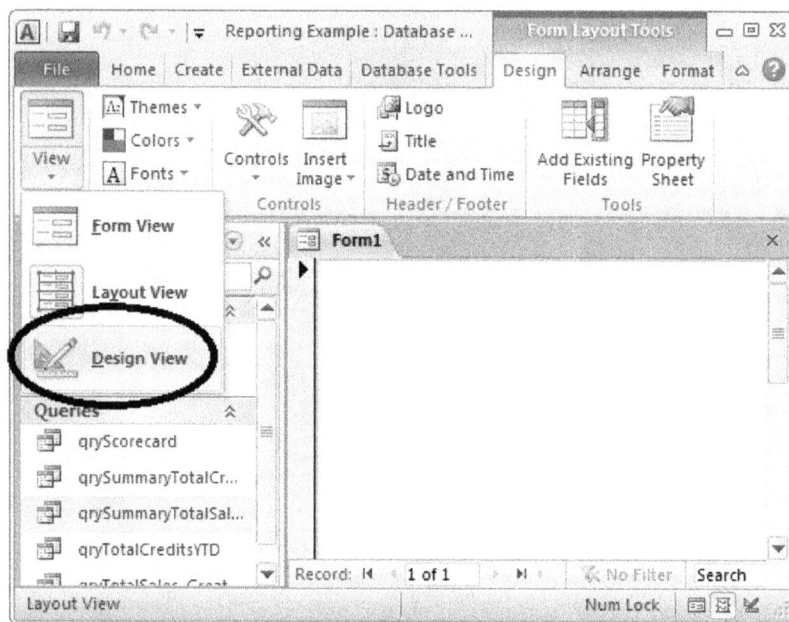

Select a button object from the ribbon, and then move your cursor to the form and draw a box with your curser. This will create a button; click cancel on the next dialog box.

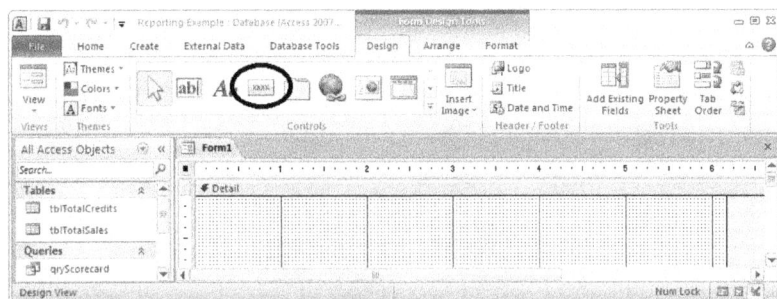

Please visit www.LetTechnologyDoTheWork.com for full image.

Double click on the button to rename it to Import Total Sales and save the form as frmMain. Create three buttons in total: Import Total Sales, Import Total Credits, and Scorecard.

We will add two statements to the import buttons: one to delete the data in the table and the other to display the table so we can add the new data.

To write a delete query, create a query and add the tblTotalSales table to the query. Then select * from the table (* means all fields) and a * will be added to the design grid. Click on X!Delete to indicate that it is a delete query. To run the query, click Run! on the ribbon, but let's not run this query now because it will delete all of the data in your table. Let's save it as qryDeleteTotalSales. We will run it from the form. In case you accidentally ran it, just copy and paste the data from the Total Sales Report (that you started with) to repopulate the table.

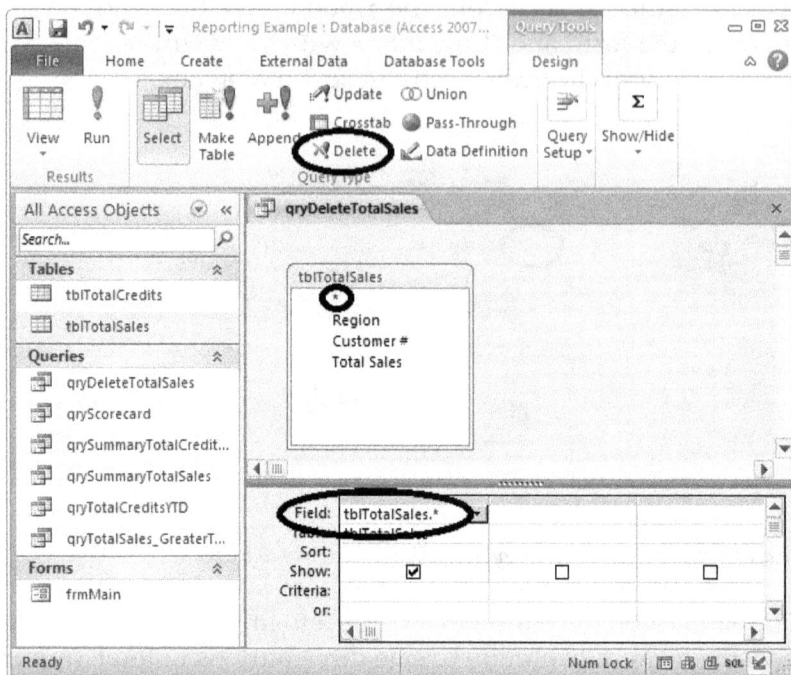

Follow the same steps to create a delete query for the Total Credits data. Save the query as qryDeleteTotalCredits.

Next, we will add the statements to the buttons. Click on frmMain to open the form, from the Home ribbon select View, Design View. Next, right click on the Import Total Sales button, select Build Event, Code Builder and OK.

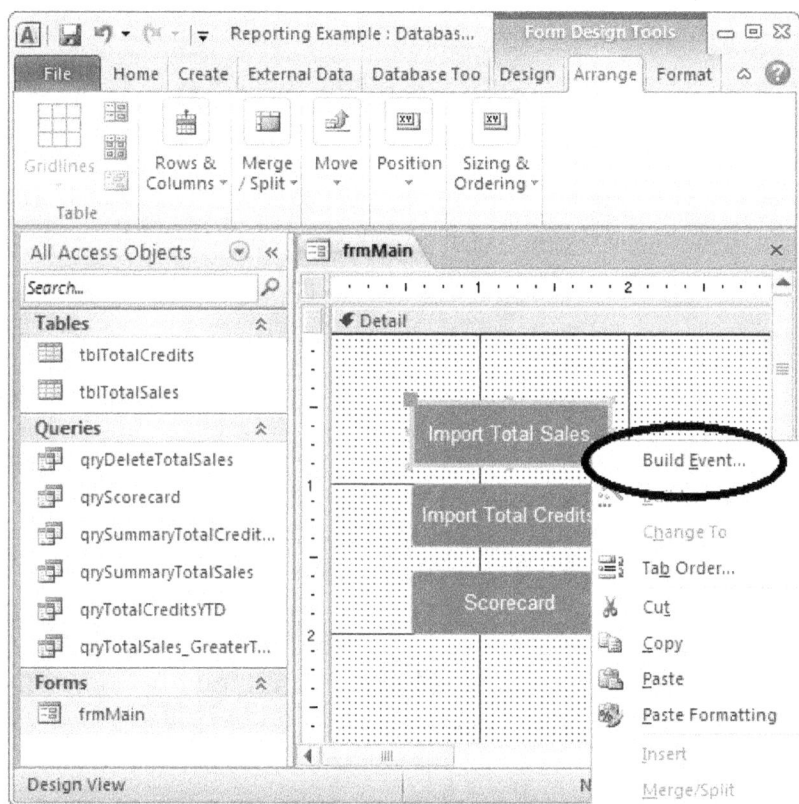

Choose Builder

Macro Builder
Expression Builder
Code Builder

OK   Cancel

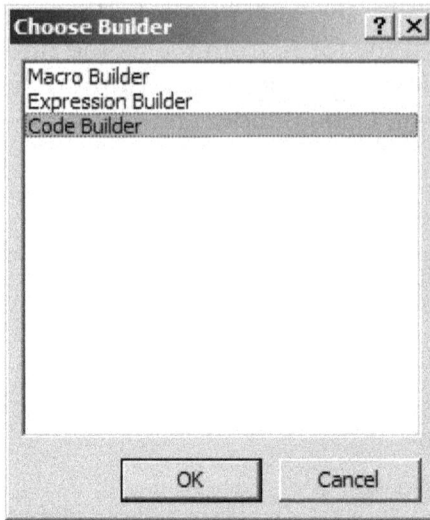

For the Import Total Sales button type the following statements between Private Sub and End Sub. Then save and close.

```
Private Sub Command0_Click()
DoCmd.OpenQuery "qryDeleteTotalSales"
DoCmd.OpenTable "tblTotalSales"
End Sub
```

For the Import Total Credits button type the following statements between Private Sub and End Sub. Then save and close.

```
Private Sub Command1_Click()
DoCmd.OpenQuery "qryDeleteTotalCredits"
DoCmd.OpenTable "tblTotalCredits"
End Sub
```

For the Scorecard button type the following statement between Private Sub and End Sub. Then save and close.

```
Private Sub Command2_Click()
DoCmd.OpenQuery "qryScorecard"
End Sub
```

For the import buttons, the first statement clears the data and the second one opens the table so you can repopulate it. The scorecard button only needs one statement to run the query. Close all of your open queries and tables.

Ideally the database will default to the main form when it opens. To set the form to default, click on File, Options, Current database Display form: frmMain.

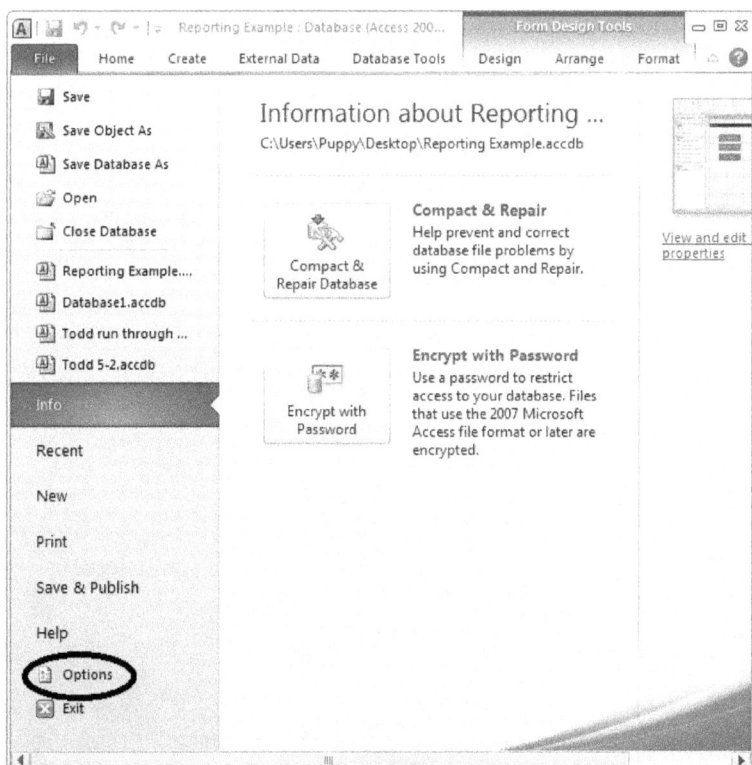

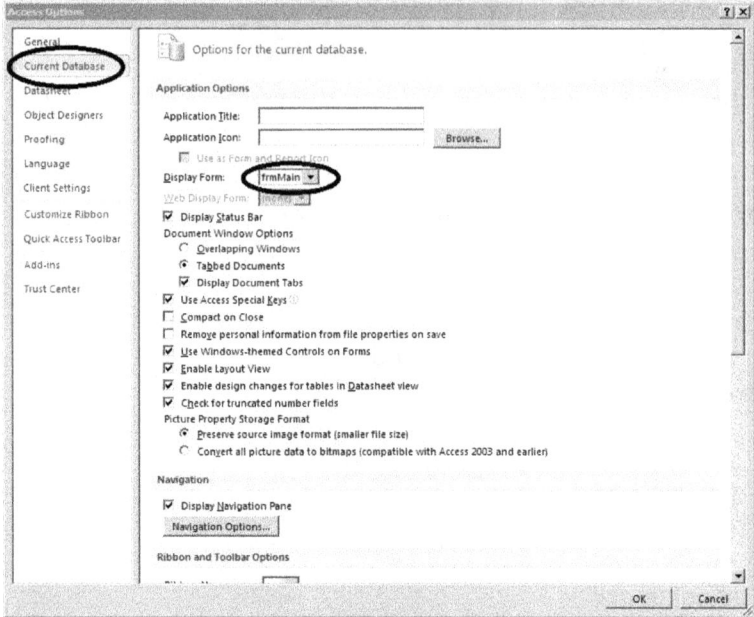

LET'S EXPERIENCE THE AUTOMATION, EXAMPLE 1: SALES AND CREDITS BY LOCATION

Now that the file is properly set up, let's run next month's data so you can see the benefits of the automation. Click on frmMain to activate the form and then Form View to activate the buttons.

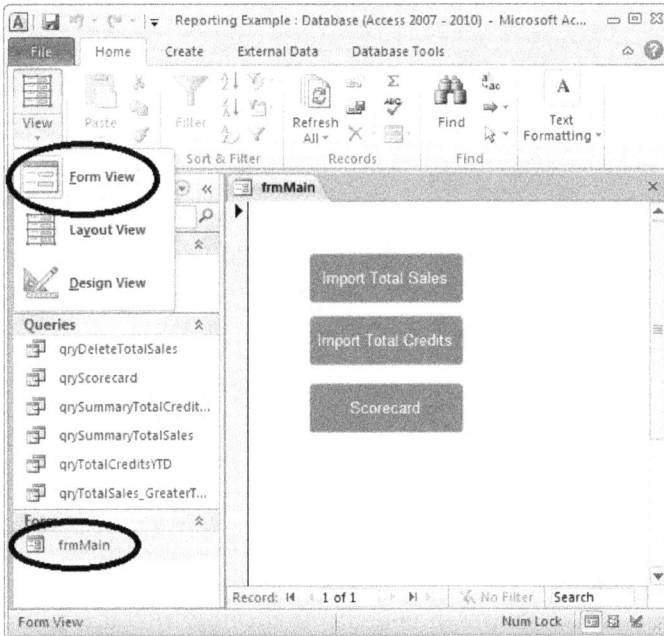

Click on the import button, Import Total Sales, and you should see the following messages:

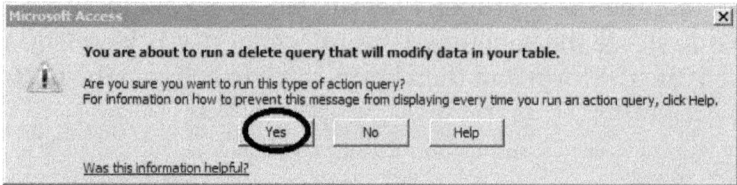

Click Yes.

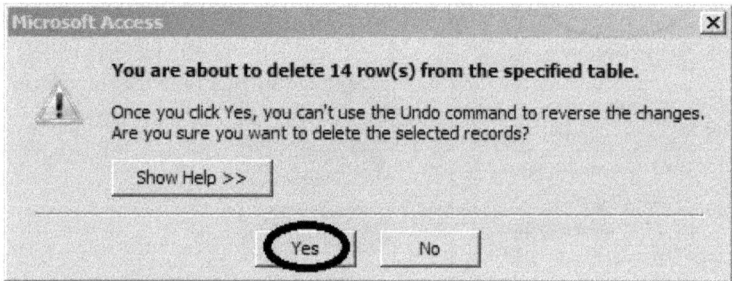

Click Yes.

The messages are just telling you that you are about to delete data. To stop the messages, add the following statement in the Code Builder:DoCmd.SetWarnings False.

```
Private Sub Command0_Click()
DoCmd.SetWarnings False
DoCmd.OpenQuery "qryDeleteTotalSales"
DoCmd.OpenTable "tblTotalSales"
End Sub
```

When the table opens, it should be blank.

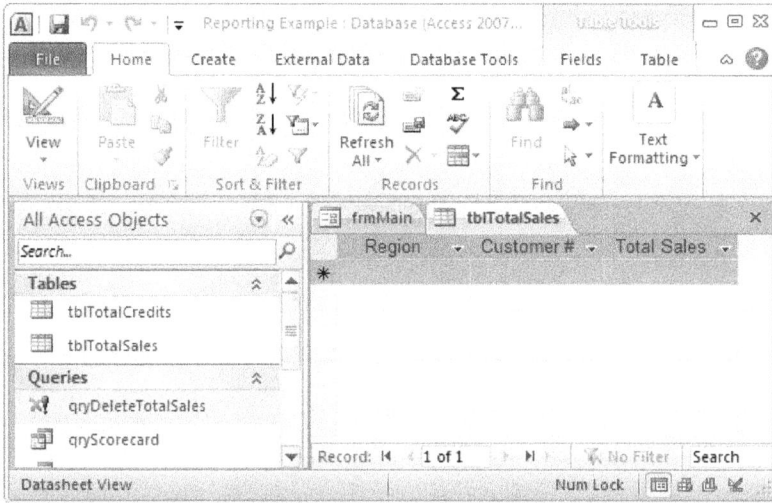

Copy/Paste the Total Sales data for the following month (in our example, use June's data) into the table. Do not include headings because we are now only populating the table. Make sure to select the entire row by clicking on the star (*) and paste the data. Follow the same steps for Total Credits data and then select the Scorecard button.

Total sales data for June. You can download the sample report at www.lettechnologydothework.com.

Region	Customer #	Total Sales
East	1	$500,000
East	2	$500,000
North	3	$40,000
North	4	$40,000
North	5	$40,000
South	6	$100,000
South	7	$20,000
South	8	$300,000
South	9	$800,000
South	10	$1,000,000
South	11	$780,000
West	12	$1,400,000
East	13	$500,000
East	14	$500,000
North	15	$40,000
North	16	$40,000
North	17	$40,000
South	18	$100,000
South	19	$20,000
South	20	$300,000
South	21	$800,000
South	22	$1,000,000
South	23	$780,000
West	24	$1,400,000

Click on the star (*) and paste the data.

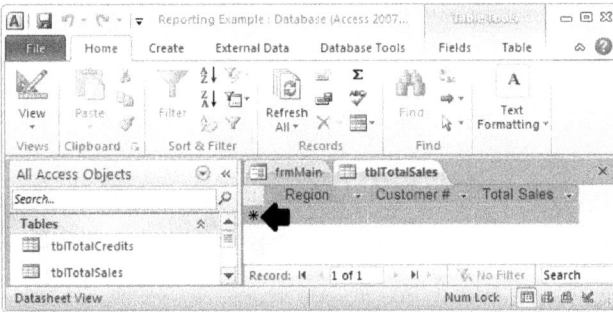

Close tblTotalSales by clicking the X in the top right corner.

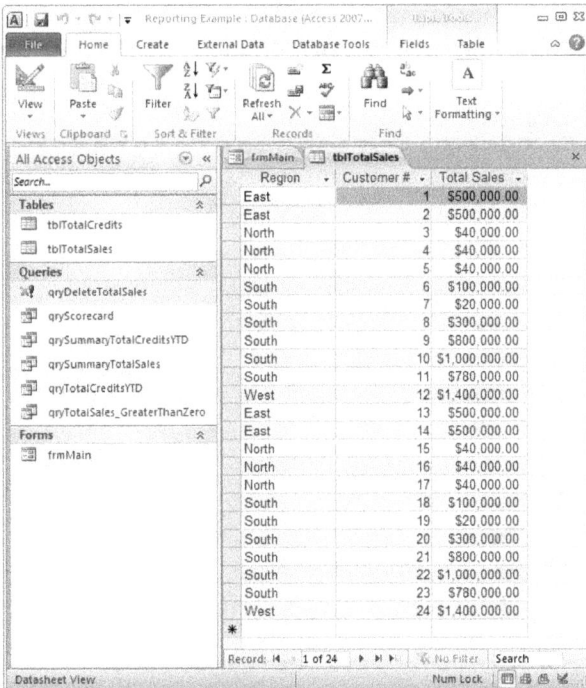

Follow the same steps for Total Credits data and then select the Scorecard button.

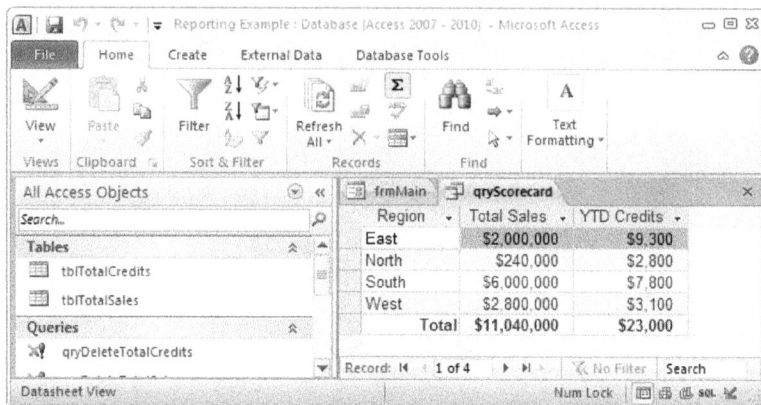

Going forward, you will only need to download the reports, click on the two import buttons, import the data, and then click on the scorecard button!

SETTING THE FILE UP, EXAMPLE 2: SALES BY REGION

Let's look at one part from Example 2: Sales by Region, mapping the regions using a different structure. This is very easy to perform in Access.

This is the Sales by Region for November with the original region structure:

Region	Location	Nov
East	NY	1200
East	CT	1800
East	MA	2400
North	MI	400
South	AL	2
South	GA	0
South	FL	800
West	AR	12
West	NV	150

Suppose this is the new structure:

Location	Region
NY	East
CT	North
MA	North
MI	Central
AL	South East
GA	South East
FL	South
CA	West
NV	Central
AR	Central

Create a new Access database and name it Reporting Example 2. Copy and paste both tables and name the first table tblSalesbyRegion and the second table tblNewRegionStructure. Create a new query and add both tables to the query. Next, link the files on location, since the region changes per location in the new structure. Select option 2 (include all records from tblSalesbyRegion and only those records from tblNewRegion Structure where the joined fields are equal) since we are only looking for regions listed on the Sales by Region table. Add the Region field from tblNewRegionStructure and the Location and Nov fields from tblSalesbyRegion to the design grid. When you run the query, you will see that locations are mapped to new regions.

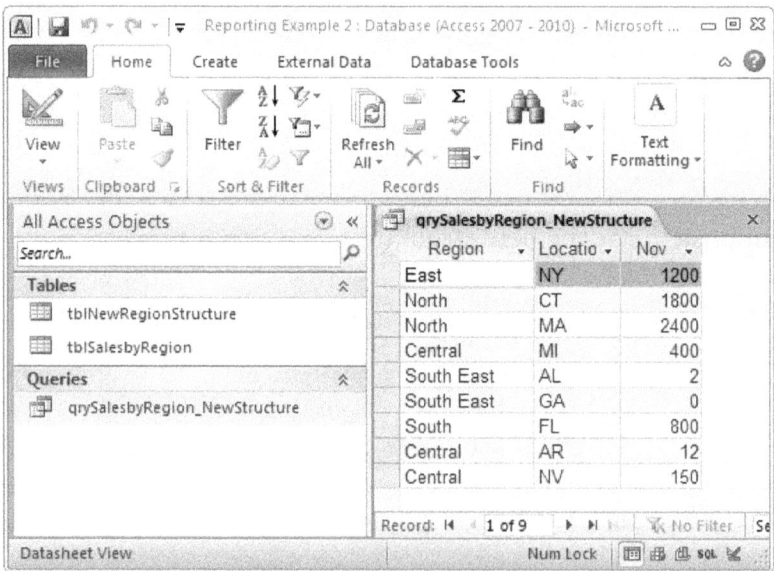

Now that you've learned a few basics on how to automate using Access, let's move on to our next chapter, Tips to Streamline Your Day.

NOTES

_____

_____

_____

_____

_____

_____

_____

_____

_____

_____

_____

_____

_____

_____

_____

_____

6
TIPS TO STREAMLINE YOUR DAY

Now that we've reviewed how automating reports can significantly reduce the amount of time that we spend on routine tasks, let's review the following tips that could help you save even more time.

If your days are anything like mine, they are jammed packed with back to back meetings, which doesn't give us much time to work on deliverables. At one point, I found myself rushing from meeting to meeting, always leaving one early to gather documents from my desk, only to be late for the next. I started feeling like my days were running me rather than the other way around. I also felt like I was not accomplishing much because I didn't have a system to track the work that I was doing between meetings or in the evening. I had to find a way to deal with this because this meeting circus seemed to be the norm. With my new system, I feel calm, less rushed, able to keep track of my ever shifting priorities, and fulfilled because I can track my daily accomplishments. The following are 14 tips from my system:

TIP 1: ORGANIZE FOLDERS & NOTES

Keep a folder for each project/major task. Using a blank piece of paper, list and number every task for each project as they arise and keep this page in the front of the folder. Staple the pages as you add them. Cross out the number of the item that you've completed—not the entire row—so you can always refer to it.

Having this information readily available will help you to remember what you've completed and reduce the amount of time that it takes to provide a status update.

Clear folders work best for me because the top sheet is visible from the outside. These top sheets will allow you to see your status at a glance, and the visibility makes it easy to pick up and table projects as priorities change with no loss of momentum. This system is also effective because everything for that project is housed in one place. No more "trying" to remember details and to-dos. Always knowing where you are on a project and what needs to done will result in less stressful projects and the ability to leave work at work.

TIP 2: CATEGORIZE EMAILS

Cleaning your inbox every day will help you feel in control of your email. First, use rules to send emails that you do not need to your deleted items, therefore avoiding your inbox. Secondly, use the categorization tasks to categorize all of your emails in your inbox. I find that this is better than adding emails to folders because I forget them when they are in folders. Categorizing emails allows me to sort by category and address all emails at once while I am working on the project. It also helps to deter me from multi-tasking. In addition, cc'ing yourself on emails that you need to follow up on keeps your emails in your inbox rather than in your sent items. Go through your emails at the end of the day, delete duplicates (where people have responded and an email chain has been created) and follow up on outstanding issues.

TIP 3: PICK A TIME TO EMAIL

Pick several times a day to email, to respond to your inbox, and resist the urge to reply every time you receive an email. Even better, shut your email off a few times a day while working on a project. This will help to prevent multi-tasking and really help you to stay in the flow. It takes about 15 minutes to get in the flow and it can be interrupted in a second. Every time your focus is interrupted, you have to get into the flow, so add these 15 minutes to everything that you are doing. You will get more done if you can keep the flow going.

TIP 4: PARE DOWN SUPPLIES

Only keep the supplies that you use every day. You can always walk over to the supplies cabinet and get more. All I really need is a ruler, pencil, pen, highlighter, stapler, and tape. Some of you may not even need these items. After paring down to only the essential items, buy a drawer divider to house these items so they are out of sight. Ensure that each item has a place in the drawer without being laid on another item. This will help you to keep your drawers organized and won't create stress when you open the drawer. Not only do messy drawers create stress for me but they also create a diversion as I feel like I have to stop what I'm doing to organize the drawer. It is always easier to find and put items away when they have a designated home. Clutter-free work areas and drawers reduce stress and allow you to focus.

TIP 5: SCHEDULE TIME FOR YOURSELF

Scheduling time for yourself is the key to feeling in control of your workload.

Blocking a half an hour or more when you arrive to the office and before you leave for the day will give you the downtime you need to get organized for the next day. Scheduling this time for yourself will help you to be more efficient and focused. During this time, categorize your emails, clean your desk, organize your folders, re-write any notes needed, and prepare for the following day's meetings. Follow these next steps to prepare for the next day:

1. Print your calendar on one page.
2. Print all supporting documents that you need for each meeting.
3. Group all items needed for each meeting and place them in a clear folder.
4. Use a post-it note and affix it to the front page of the folder with the name of the meeting, conference room if applicable, and time.
5. Stack all folders together, placing the calendar on top.

Now you are prepared for your meetings and can enjoy a stress-free evening knowing that you are ready for the next day's activities. This will also help you when you are rushing from meeting to meeting. You will have everything that you need with you so you don't have to stop at your desk.

TIP 6: ONE FOLDER ON YOUR HARD DRIVE

Have you ever had to hunt and peck for a file on your desktop during a meeting and feel flustered? I feel flustered just watching someone do this. Having a clean and organized filing system will help you to find files faster.

Keep one folder on your hard drive in order to reduce clutter. Then create subfolders for each project or major task that you are working on and an admin folder (benefits, notes, etc.). Having one folder on your desktop allows for:

1. The flexibility to change computers quickly by only having to move one folder.
2. Make efficient backups.

3. Search for files using the search function, as you only need to select one folder. The search function will search all subfolders.
4. Gives you the confidence of knowing that all of your files are in one place.

I save all of my files to either a shared drive, if other people need to access them, or the one on my desktop. Some companies provide a private folder on the network that only you can access. I recommend saving as many files as possible here instead of your desktop if your company offers this because the company will perform routine backups of this folder so you don't have to do it manually. I also change the icons so I can find folders quickly.

TIP 7: SET REMINDERS

If you don't have an accurate internal clock, then setting reminders is the key in keeping your day on track. I set multiple reminders:

Reminder 1: 5 am wakeup
Reminder 2: 6:30 am get ready for work
Reminder 3: 7:30 am leave for work
Reminder 4: 4:30 pm wrap up and prepare for tomorrow
Reminder 5: 5:30 pm leave work and go to the gym
Reminder 6: 7:00 pm start dinner
Reminder 7: 9:00 pm go to bed

Sometimes I get so entrenched in an activity that I lose track of time. Setting alarms keeps me on track and ensures that I am prepared for the following day.

TIP 8: IF YOU MISS YOUR WINDOW, LET IT GO

If you miss a preplanned window of an activity, let it go; otherwise, you will always be playing catch up. For instance, if I work late and get home at 6:30 pm, then I go on to dinner. I don't try to catch up on the gym and then make dinner because then the rest of my day will be condensed, and I will stay up too late and throw off the following day. If this continues to happen, it could be a sign that you need to adjust your schedule.

TIP 9: EDIT, DELETE, SHRED, AND SCAN

Edit, edit, edit! Delete and shred. Throw away anything that you don't need. This will help to reduce the amount of paper in your office and will allow you to keep your office organized. Nowadays, items are usually emailed or downloaded, so you can save them to a folder rather than keeping paper. If the item is only in paper, then scan it and save it on your computer. Once a month, go through your folders (paper and on the computer) and delete the items that you have completed or don't need any more. Having less paper and files will allow you to focus on the items that you need to finish. There is nothing more frustrating than looking for files or trying to figure out which file is the latest version.

TIP 10: TOMORROW'S FOCUS LIST

During your wrap up time at the end of the day, write 3 priority items down that you will address the next day on a blank sheet of paper (or calendar) and leave it on your desk so you see it first thing in the morning. This could include following up with people, projects, or even tasks. Chances are we won't complete more than 3 items a day and seeing a laundry list of items that we cannot get to first thing in the morning will cause more stress throughout the day. One priority item may be comprised of many subtasks, which are referenced in the individual folders (see Tip 1 Organize Folders & Notes). For example, if I am addressing issues in a system, I'll write the system on my list that triggers me to go to that project folder. Then I'll start working down the list of items listed on the front sheet of the project.

TIP 11: ONLY KEEP THINGS ON YOUR DESK THAT YOU ARE WORKING ON

Due to the increasing pressures and the multiple demands onour days, we are all tempted to multi-task. Multi-tasking pulls our focus away from our projects and usually results in being less efficient. The only thing you should have on your desk is the project that you are working on. If you are having a hard time focusing on this project because you are constantly reminding yourself of open items on other projects, write them down so you can address them later. Part of our stress comes from trying to remind ourselves not to forget to do something. Writing it down will ensure that we don't forget and clears our mind.

TIP 12: GROUP FOLDERS BY PRIORITY

Categorize and group each folder by priority. You can use rubber bands or baskets to keep priorities together. This will prevent you from going through your folders every day and reminding yourself of all of the outstanding items that haven't been addressed. Worrying about them won't let you get to them any quicker but addressing your current folder and completing it will. Focus all of your efforts on one project, complete it, and then move to your next top priority. This will also organize your projects by priority so you can easily discuss them with your manager during your next prioritization meeting.

TIP 13: UPDATE THE STATUS OF PROJECTS OFTEN

Create a template that addresses the following: budget (hours or money, or both), what you have accomplished, roadblocks, and items needed to finish task. Before you move on to another project, update this status and keep it in your file. This will allow you to provide a status quickly and accurately and to prepare for performance reviews when that time comes around. It will also help you to keep track of your projects so you can escalate issues such as communicating budget overages.

TIP 14: FOCUS ENERGY ON TASKS THAT ARE IMPORTANT

Review the tasks that you completed at the end of the week to ensure that they align with the priorities that your manager has communicated to you. If you are off course, this is the time to realign. The longer we deviate from our priorities, the more stress it will create. Performing this review weekly will help to close this gap quickly.

Now that we've reviewed how to organize your day, let's discuss some tips to automate everyday life.

NOTES

_____

_____

_____

_____

_____

_____

_____

_____

_____

_____

_____

_____

_____

_____

_____

_____

7
OUTSOURCE IT!

We've covered automating reports and tips for organizing our work days. Now, let's review how we can reduce the time we spend on routine tasks at home. Technology is amazing because it has afforded us the luxury of getting an enormous amount of information at one time; however, it has also increased the complexity of our everyday lives. We get information from many different sources. For example, TV, podcasts, TEDTalks, work email, home email, just to name a few. Our phones are constantly going off with text messages, emails and push notifications. I know we all try not to look, but you have to be very disciplined in order to let all of that go. In order to balance the increased complexity of our lives and to achieve our goals in a limited amount of time, there are a number of things that we can outsource. There are a lot of items that many people already outsource like yard work or auto repairs, but I found a few more non-conventional outsourcing opportunities that you may want to try. Not all of these outsourcing strategies are for everyone, but I thought I'd point out additional services that may interest you.

NUTRITIONIST

Being healthy increases energy and allows us to focus and accomplish so much more. I was spending a lot of time researching what to eat, what vitamins to take, and the timing of meals. There was so much to consider that I noticed that I was starting to deprioritize it because I didn't have the time to wrap my arms around everything, so I decided to consult with a nutrition expert. A nutrition expert stays on top of current nutrition needs and can summarize, customize, and disseminate the information to you, saving you many hours of researching. I contact her every few months to ensure that I am staying on track and to see if I need to tweak anything. I probably spend a total of 2 hours with her throughout the year over the phone. She has become my go-to expert when I am feeling a little off balance. She usually recommends changes to my diet or vitamins, and I'm back to feeling energized in a few days. My nutritionist has really helped me to increase my focus throughout the day so I am able to accomplish the tasks that I set out to do.

THIRD PARTY GROCERY DELIVERY

I started using a grocery delivery service a few years ago and love it! Instead of going to the grocery store, I hop online, order my groceries, and select a delivery time. This allows me the freedom to do my grocery shopping at any time. For instance, I can shop online at night and request that my groceries are delivered before breakfast.

DINNER DELIVERY SERVICE

I use a dinner delivery service when I am at the office during dinner time. There are several dinner delivery service companies and they all service different areas and restaurants. I used to go out and pick dinner up and found that it would take me an hour and a half to get focused again. Now I order online, and it arrives in about an hour with minimal disruption.

PERSONAL CHEF

A personal chef can save you a significant amount of time every week. Some chefs go grocery shopping, cook your meals in their commissary kitchen, and then deliver them once a week. Other chefs will cook in your home, package the meals, and clean the kitchen.

This is a huge time saver as you will no longer have to go to the grocery store, cook from scratch every evening, and clean up the kitchen. Or, if you are like me, cook for a full day to prepare meals for the week. You can provide the list that the nutritionist gives you to the personal chef to ensure that you are eating healthy meals. Sometimes if you don't have the energy or time to cook, it's easier to just eat out but it is usually not healthy and can be expensive over time.

Personal chefs are usually flexible when it comes to packaging your meals. You can ask for meals in larger containers for dinner and/or in lunch size containers so you are ready for lunch every day. This will significantly reduce the amount of time that it takes you to get your lunch ready for work.

DRY CLEANING SERVICE

Some dry cleaners are very flexible and will come to your house to pick your dry cleaning up and drop it off once a week. Having your dry cleaning on a schedule is very helpful because your dry cleaning doesn't pile up, and you always have clothes ready and pressed for the following week. Asking your dry cleaner to come to your house will reduce the number of errands that you need to run during the week.

PERSONAL ASSISTANT

There are personal assistants that you can hire on an hourly basis. These personal assistants can run most errands for you. This can include grocery shopping, clothes shopping, returning items, etc.

PROFESSIONAL ORGANIZERS

Professional organizers can help you organize your home so you can become more efficient. They can organize everyday life or help you with specific projects. Some of these projects may include organizing storage units, closets, the kitchen, scanning items, etc. Sometimes some of these projects are just too overwhelming for us to tackle after working a full week, and we just need a little bit of help to finish them.

CLOTHING STYLIST

Stylists are amazing. A stylist can come to your house and help you to clean out your closet. You can try on all of your clothes and they can tell you what fits and what colors look good on you. They will also take notes and see what pieces you are missing. Then you can schedule a shopping trip to shop for the pieces.

There are many people that are starting to lean towards a personal uniform or a capsule wardrobe in order to reduce the number of decisions that need to be made in the morning. This can also be achieved by hiring a stylist that selects pieces that all go together. Having a closet full of pieces that go together helps you to get ready in the morning quickly and stress free, because you can just pick anything out of your closet and look put together.

Working with a stylist significantly reduces the amount of time that you spend shopping every year. They usually shop for your items before you meet with them and have everything ready in the dressing rooms so you can just go from store to store to try the items on and buy them. Since the stylist already knows the clothes that are out there, you can usually buy everything in one shopping trip, lasting approximately three hours. Another benefit of having a stylist is if you find that you need an item during the year, you can email them for a recommendation, saving you time because you don't have to research what you're looking for.

Not only do stylists reduce the amount of time that you spend shopping every year, but they also select pieces that are classic that you will actually wear. There is nothing more frustrating than having a full closet and feeling like you don't have anything to wear.

Stylists can work on any budget. I wasted money every time I bought something I couldn't wear but a stylist can help you avoid this. Limiting the number of shopping trips a year can help you stick to your budget. For example, if you shop with a stylist twice a year — in May for spring/summer and in October for fall/winter — then you are only spending money twice rather than buying constantly throughout the year.

CAR CLEANING

There are several companies that will come to your house or office to clean your car. Normally when you bring your car in on the weekend, you have to wade through traffic, sit and wait for your car to be cleaned, and then sit in traffic on the way home. This can save a lot of time depending on how often you get your car cleaned.

HOUSEKEEPING

Having a house keeper will reduce the amount of time that you spend cleaning your house every week. It will also help reduce the amount of items that you have in your house if the house keeper brings their cleaning supplies with them. It is much easier to have a clean house all of the time if the house keeper comes once a week. You can usually negotiate with a housekeeper to reduce the rate depending on how often they come.

These are just a few outsourcing services that could help you to save time at home. I am always looking for more outsourcing services. If you are using a service that saves you time at home, please visit my website at www.lettechnologydothework.com and submit your idea. Ideas are always welcome!

WHAT'S NEXT

Now that you have learned how to save time with these tips, you should begin feeling more productive at work and at home and have a little extra time to enjoy the things that you love to do outside of the office. Be sure to download the sample reports at www.lettechnologydothework.com. I'd love to hear how *Let Technology Do the Work* has helped you.

NOTES

About the Author

Eva Madison lives in Atlanta, GA with her husband Todd. She has held positions in audit, reporting and analysis, system integration and data management. She has undergraduate degrees in Accounting and Information Systems. She also has an MBA from Emory and is a CPA.

www.ingramcontent.com/pod-product-compliance
Lightning Source LLC
Chambersburg PA
CBHW071904200326
41519CB00016B/4503